THE

BOLD TRUTH

ABOUT MUTUAL FUNDS

THE

BOLD TRUTH

ABOUT MUTUAL FUNDS

BY ADAM BOLD
Founder and CEO of The Mutual Fund Store
Creator and host of The Mutual Fund Show on radio

WITH MARTIN ROSENBERG

ROCKHILL
BOOKS

The Bold Truth about Mutual Funds

By Adam Bold
Founder and CEO of The Mutual Fund Store
Creator and host of The Mutual Fund Show on radio

With Martin Rosenberg

Published by Rockhill Books,
an imprint of The Kansas City Star
1729 Grand Boulevard
Kansas City, Missouri 64108

BOOK
AND COVER
DESIGN:
SUZANNE C.
HURTIG

COVER
PHOTOGRAPHS:
REBECCA
FRIEND-JIMENEZ

EDITOR:
DOUG
WEAVER

First edition, first printing
ISBN: 0-9764021-0-6

Printed in the United States of America by
Walsworth Publishing Co., Inc.
Marceline, Missouri

*To order copies, call StarInfo (816-234-4636 and
say "operator.") www.TheKansasCityStore.com*

DEDICATION

For my Dad, who taught me
what it means to be a gentleman.

TABLE
o f
CONTENTS

INTRODUCTION

My first introduction to Adam Bold came during my stint as business editor of *The Kansas City Star.* Our staff was organizing a MoneyWise Fair, a two-day show at our city's convention center where the public and investment advisers could come together and talk money.

Adam was a fledgling entrepreneur at the time. He'd just started a little business called The Mutual Fund Store out in the suburbs. He was young, bright, likeable and knowledgeable. Adam also showed some marketing finesse. Knowing he'd need to cut through the clutter of all the other investment advisers in town, Adam began hosting a radio show each Saturday that played on a local station. He'd take calls from average-joe investors about their mutual funds. It was a hit.

So on this weekend, Adam decided to do his Saturday-morning show from the MoneyWise Fair floor. And he asked to interview me. No problem,

I thought. I'm no marketing genius, but I, too, see the value of free airtime.

After a few niceties, Adam, in rapid-fire fashion, got right to the point: "So, Doug, as business editor, what's it going to take to get all mutual funds listed in your newspaper? How come you're only listing some...not all? Don't you realize that mutual funds are the fastest-growing investment vehicle among average investors? Don't you see that you're short-changing your readers? *The Wall Street Journal* can do it, why can't you?"

Ouch. After plodding through my usual explanation of the high cost of newsprint, we said our good-byes, and Adam went back to taking calls from listeners.

I left bruised but impressed. Here was a guy who clearly was an advocate for the mutual-fund investor. And after listening to his radio show over the years, I'm now convinced that he's a sane and objective voice amid a cacophony of mutual-fund noise that's so prevalent in the trade today.

Let me make it clear: Adam is in business to make money. His Mutual Fund Store concept is growing quickly in cities across the country. His listener base for his radio show is widening at the same time. It's a one-two punch...a powerful and fruitful combination.

But Adam is doing good at the same time. He takes no prisoners when calling the fund industry

LET ME MAKE IT CLEAR: ADAM IS IN BUSINESS TO MAKE MONEY. BUT ADAM IS DOING GOOD AT THE SAME TIME. HE TAKES NO PRISONERS WHEN CALLING THE FUND INDUSTRY TO TASK FOR ITS ETHICAL LAPSES.

to task for its ethical lapses. He absolutely shreds any pretense that brokers are conflict-free when it comes to looking out for your best interests. And he teaches. Every week, his voice is piped to thousands of listeners, hammering home key points:

- o Make an investment plan.
- o Stick to that plan.
- o Avoid load funds.
- o Avoid annuities.
- o Know your investment adviser—and better still, know how he makes his money.
- o Most important, know yourself.

It's sound advice.

This book is Adam's first attempt to gather all of his thoughts and put them into a cohesive whole. It's instructive and provocative at the same time. But that's what good self-help books do...spur you to act, then offer guideposts for the journey.

Enjoy *The Bold Truth About Mutual Funds*. You'll learn some things. I did.

Doug Weaver
Publisher, Rockhill Books
Kansas City, Missouri

CHAPTER ONE

Who I Am

"HI, BILL. THIS IS ADAM BOLD. WHAT'S YOUR QUESTION?"

"Well, I am a passive investor. That is, for the last 15 years I've been with the same account exec with a large firm, one of the biggest that was fined recently. He put me in some mutual funds and I wake up later on and decide that I'm really not getting much of a return. So, I'm wondering how I can become a more active investor and where I can find a list of the mutual funds that I probably should be in since his advice isn't making due. I guess that's the reason why I'm listening to your station."

W HO I AM

My work, my passion, is my business: helping others to invest wisely. Where did those motivations come from? I, like many others, have been shaped by family. What may be unique in my case, however, is the specific, clear direction given to me from my earliest conscious moments. I was destined to become an accountant. I come by that almost genetically. My dad was a certified public accountant and a tax attorney. Both of my grandfathers were CPAs. My great-grandfather, the oldest child in his family, had to learn a trade when he landed in the Midwest around 1900. So he became an accountant and set up shop in the bustling heart of Kansas City, Kansas, in the middle of America. Interestingly, he worked from an office located in the same building where two brothers set up a rival firm that was destined to become the tax preparation giant, H&R Block.

I started working at my grandfather's accounting practice when I was about 12 years old, reporting for duty during summers. Because

The Bold Truth About Mutual Funds

he was my grandfather, the job interview went well. I started out reconciling bank accounts. A business would turn over a big package of 1,000 checks they had written that month, and I put them in numerical order and then reconciled the bank account. I entered bookkeeping journal entries in a ledger book; I worked on payroll, income statements and other vital records. When I was old enough to drive, I visited businesses scattered across the city to pick up their books for updating. We served many independent grocers who put in long hours building up their neighborhood shops. We also served car dealers and manufacturers. The work may have been tedious but was invaluable. I learned from an early age the importance of understanding financial statements and financial issues.

I also gained a valuable insight into some truths about stock-picking. Not only did we do the books for various companies, but we would do personal taxes for their owners and officers. I saw quite frequently that most of those people who actively traded stocks lost money. It was common to see people with successful businesses making heaps of money routinely lose 20 percent of the value of their stock portfolio— and, of course, sometimes much more.

I worked for my grandfather for several years after attending college and training to be an accountant. But my grandfather's retirement

> **I SAW QUITE FREQUENTLY THAT MOST OF THOSE PEOPLE WHO ACTIVELY TRADED STOCKS LOST MONEY.**

forced me in a new direction. He always vowed that he would never retire. But then, one day in 1991, he literally woke up and said, "You know, I don't feel like going to work today." He told me, "I'm going to sell my practice. I don't know if you want it, but you can have it."

NOT FOR ME

The truth was, I didn't enjoy the business. I couldn't see myself behind a desk reading columns of numbers my entire business career. Aspects of accounting could be really interesting. My grandfather's practice, however, focused on bookkeeping and payroll records and taxes. I politely declined the offer. It is worth noting what happened to his business after he sold it to a large firm in 1991. My grandfather had an instinct for how much it costs to take care of a particular client. Every year he would charge a little more. The large firm that acquired his practice, employing modern business practices, quickly ramped up its charges. Within a year and a half, the firm lost 90 percent of the business volume it had purchased from my grandfather.

But that was not my worry. In 1991, at age 27, I was set to embark on a new adventure. I went to work with the venerable Wall Street institution of Smith Barney, which is now the third largest brokerage house. By then, I was married to my wife Sharon, a nurse, and she was pregnant with our first child. I was ready to find my place in the world. The world of investments always intrigued me. Both my father and grandfather were investors and greatly influenced me. I was given stock when I was born. At dinner, my family would often discuss investments and world events. When I joined Smith Barney, it was a different firm than it is today; it had 2,500 brokers nationwide who catered to very high net-worth individuals. One acquaintance, a branch manager, compared brokerages at the time to auto manufacturers. Merrill Lynch, like Chevrolet, wanted to appeal to everyone. Smith Barney, like a Mercedes, appealed to the elite.

I went to work for Smith Barney believing I knew more about the markets than the average guy. I quickly learned, however, that I didn't know anything about being a stock broker. Smith Barney sent me to New York for six weeks of training. What was interesting, in hindsight, about that training was they didn't teach me a lot about investments or how to be capable of making good investment decisions. They taught me how to *sell* investments. They brought in some product people who would explain a little bit about commodities, municipal bonds, mutual funds or stocks. That was about maybe a third of our training. The balance of our training dealt with how to sell. One man did nothing but

I WENT TO WORK FOR SMITH BARNEY BELIEVING I KNEW MORE ABOUT THE MARKETS THAN THE AVERAGE GUY. I QUICKLY LEARNED, HOWEVER, THAT I DIDN'T KNOW ANYTHING ABOUT BEING A STOCK BROKER.

teach us how to "cold call." We spent probably about half our time with the calling guru. We all quickly got the message that cold calling was central to being a broker.

THE DRILL

Here's how it worked: I'd land at my desk in the morning and make 1,000 dials before lunch, to get to talk to 100 people, to get 10 prospects, to get one client. Most of the time, the prospect's secretary wouldn't let me through to the boss, or a phone number was busy, or nobody answered. After lunch I would make 1,000 more calls. I would buy the lists of phone numbers, or the branch manager would buy them. One list might include the names of individuals who owned at least $50,000 worth of investments; another might list subscribers to Money magazine; a third might hold the names of people who own private planes. All day long, I'd sit with a headset in a cubicle. Back in those days it was really hard. Now it would be next to impossible because of the "do not call" lists and other restrictions. I kind of caught the tail end of the cold-calling era.

At Smith Barney, we had probably 60 people in this first training class. Two months later, we lost about half the class because they couldn't handle the rigor of the routine. Others left because they couldn't stand to lose money for

> I'D LAND AT MY DESK IN THE MORNING AND MAKE 1,000 DIALS BEFORE LUNCH, TO GET TO TALK TO 100 PEOPLE, TO GET 10 PROSPECTS, TO GET ONE CLIENT.

their clients. They would sell a client an investment for $10,000, it would drop in value to $8,000, and they couldn't face talking to the client again.

I proved to be a better-than-average salesperson. I was ranked among the top three students in my class of 60. I had a six-figure income, which was not bad for someone just starting out. Things were going swimmingly. Over time, however, Smith Barney changed. In 1994, Smith Barney bought Shearson Lehman and went from 2,500 brokers to 11,500 brokers. The next year, it bought Solomon Brothers and increased its staff to 14,000 brokers. The whole nature of the firm changed. Up until that point, I would sit with a potential client and say, "What do you want? What do you need? Let me try to find a strategy that will meet your needs." But Smith Barney began to tell us what to sell. So they would come to me and say, "We are bringing out the Smith Barney XYZ Fund, and we expect you to sell $1 million worth of the fund."

About the same time, I started getting calls from headhunters. I knew I needed to work for someone else—a company that hadn't been through these mergers and didn't do business this way. I moved on to Prudential Securities for awhile. But it still wasn't a good fit. I realized I needed to head in an entirely new direction.

> THEY WOULD SELL A CLIENT AN INVESTMENT FOR **$10,000**, IT WOULD DROP IN VALUE TO **$8,000**, AND THEY COULDN'T FACE TALKING TO THE CLIENT AGAIN.

As I was maturing as a broker, I gained an important insight. I discovered that I love helping people with their investments. As time went by, I became better and better at it. Over time, I had an extended network of clients. I had the advantage of being the fifth generation of my family in Kansas City. My father had ownership in a couple of banks. I sat in on the loan committee meetings with him. In addition to making many contacts, I learned a lot about how business worked. The loan officers would come in and say, "A group of dentists needs a loan." We would look through their books. I got to see how all these different businesses operated and which ones were profitable and which ones weren't and how money was made.

> SMITH BARNEY WOULD COME TO ME AND SAY, "WE ARE BRINGING OUT THE SMITH BARNEY XYZ FUND, AND WE EXPECT YOU TO SELL $1 MILLION WORTH OF THE FUND."

THE DAWNING

The concept for The Mutual Fund Store came as an epiphany: I could build a business around selling mutual funds. In the brokerage industry I was selling load funds, because that was all we were allowed to sell. It wasn't as much fun, and I didn't make as much money selling mutual funds as I did trading stock. It dawned on me, though, that over the long run, clients holding mutual funds, if they were decent funds, had earned a much better return than clients buying and selling individual stocks. I was making a lot

CASE STUDY NO. 1

A couple with three grown children came to us with an interesting, although not unique, situation. Two of the couple's children were responsible, maintained well-paying, secure jobs, and had long demonstrated the ability to manage their finances. But the third child was never able to keep a job or handle money. The couple was in their late 60s and was looking to set up a trust for their children but were understandably concerned about how the third child would handle his sizeable inheritance.

The client needed to set up a strategic plan that would allow each of the three children to receive their money in a manner that would be appropriate for their situation. Since the three people had shown different abilities to deal with money, the estate should be structured so each of them would be treated in a different manner. In the end a plan was structured that allowed the two responsible children access to the estate but limited the third to an annual withdrawal equal to his income for that year.

CONCLUSION

Creative planning can resolve just about any issue. When you are confronted with a situation that has unique challenges or obstacles, look for innovative ways to meet your goals. Individual situations require individual solutions, and creative investing and planning will allow you to meet your goals.

more money from the stock clients. But clients in mutual funds were more successful in building their wealth. I decided to provide advice on mutual funds for a fee instead of selling whatever I could get someone to buy on a transactional basis.

So it came to me all at once, in the middle of the night in 1995: I would open The Mutual Fund Store.

In 1996, computers were about to totally transform the investment world. One of the things that helped me be successful at Smith Barney and at Prudential was that I learned how to make the most of computer technology early on. It allowed me to keep track of clients and their holdings in a unique way. I have always been a big believer that there are tools that can help me do my job more effectively. Prior to the explosive growth of the Internet less than a decade ago, if you wanted to get stock quotes you had to contact a broker. My clients couldn't just get stock quotes anywhere; they had to call me to obtain them. There was no CNBC.

I realized, however, that with the Internet I could start my own business and get stock quotes and have access to this information in a way that an independent adviser could not have had just 10 years earlier. I discussed my vision of a mutual fund store with my father. He said it would never work. There have been very few times in my life when my father's advice hasn't been right. Fortunately in this case, I said, "Dad, you know I am going to go ahead and do it." As is the case with many new businesses, after awhile I ran out of capital. No banks would make me a loan. Ultimately, I had to go my dad and borrow money, and he was extremely gracious about it. His generosity was invaluable in getting me through.

The first two years, the business grew slowly, starting from a base of about 100 loyal clients I had brought with me from the brokerage houses. Blastoff occurred in early 1998, when I landed my own radio broadcast on Kansas City radio station KCMO. My "big break" in radio came when a local accountant, Peter Newman, had a three-hour Saturday morning show called Money Line. One day he invited me on as a guest. We hit it off and produced good radio. A month later, he invited me back. Over time I started being on the show every other week. When he would go on vacation, I would host the show. Eventually, the station invited me to host a one-hour program of my own at 10 a.m. I will forever be indebted to Peter for helping me get my start in radio.

My business grew from $10 million under management in 1997 to $50 million by the end of 1998. That was a good time in the market, and certainly some of my success is due to lucky timing. But I also had a message that was different from what investors were accustomed to hearing—in either good or bad times. My message from the start has been very client-focused instead of commission-focused. People responded.

> **I** REALIZED THAT WITH THE **INTERNET I** COULD START MY OWN BUSINESS AND GET STOCK QUOTES AND HAVE ACCESS TO THIS INFORMATION IN A WAY THAT AN INDEPENDENT ADVISOR COULD NOT HAVE HAD JUST **10** YEARS EARLIER.

In 1999, I received a call from a prospective
client, John Young. As I did with all new clients, I
sat with him and explained what we do and how
we do it. He immediately opened an account for a
large six figure sum. The next day he

CASE STUDY No. 2

*A potential client who had become disappointed with the performance
of her investments came to see us about reformulating her portfolio.
The client owned a large number of "B" share Putnam funds and in
addition to her unhappiness with the movement of the funds she
had developed some concerns about unethical behavior Putnam was
involved in. She was looking to move her money to a fund where
neither of those issues would be a concern.*

*The problem she faced was withdrawing or moving her "B" funds would
result in a penalty of about $8000. After watching the funds under-
perform for a period of time she was reluctant to absorb even more of
a loss. The client was in a very disappointing position, but she decided
to transfer the funds, take the financial hit, and begin working towards
recouping her losses and improving her position.*

CONCLUSION

*When you realize that you are in a bad situation take action to correct
it, even if it involves some short-term losses. It is difficult to acknowl-
edge a mistake and bite the bullet, but successful investment involves
risk and positioning. If you recognize that you are in a bad position or
are taking a poor risk get out of it and try to find a better investment.*

called me back and said that he loved my concept and that he and his partner in a venture capital firm, Jim Abrams, wanted to help take my business nationwide.

At the time, I was working more than 12 hours a day. I would get to work at 8:30, work until 6 p.m., go home and have dinner, return at 7:30 p.m. and work until 11 p.m. I would do that five days a week and then go in on Saturday and do the radio show. There was just no way that I could work on a national expansion and run my day-to-day business. So I told John and Jim that I was not ready. Periodically, they would ask me about my plans.

Eventually, the business starting doing really well, and I was able to start hiring people to help out. Jon Bentz, my chief opera-tions officer, joined us and started running the business. He structured the back office, and we hired people to do the portfolio accounting, print out statements and print out presentations. I hired additional advisers to meet with clients.

Finally, I was in a position to team up with Young and Abrams and their firm, VenVest, Inc. We formed a partnership in 2000. There are a lot of venture capitalists who put money into a deal and then try to sell out in a year or two. Jim and John are different; these guys are business builders.

> MY MESSAGE FROM THE START HAS BEEN VERY CLIENT-FOCUSED INSTEAD OF COMMISSION-FOCUSED. PEOPLE RESPONDED.

GROWTH PATH

The first thing we did was open a second store in St. Louis. I had built a great business in Kansas City, but I was also there nurturing it every day. The question was whether it would work somewhere I wasn't. I launched a radio program in the summer of 2000. It worked like a charm. I built a small, cozy broadcast studio in the back of my Overland Park, Kan., store and used high-speed telephone lines to the Kansas City and St. Louis radio stations. Now we have so many stations on our network that we connect through the Westwood One Satellite Network.

The broadcasts are sheer fun. I talk to interesting people and express my views—on everything from where the economy is headed to the scandals that have recently rocked the mutual fund industry. I've worked very hard over the years to be good on the radio; I've sought training from every professional radio personality that would take the time to teach me.

The combination of offering carefully tailored advice to clients in The Mutual Fund Store and explaining sound investment principles to a mass audience via radio is my calling. I love it—and I think I am good at it. Today we are in about 20 markets. In five years I hope to see Mutual Fund Stores in the top 100 markets in the country, including a local radio show for each one of them.

> THE BROAD-CASTS ARE SHEER FUN. I TALK TO INTERESTING PEOPLE AND EXPRESS MY VIEWS—ON EVERYTHING FROM WHERE THE ECONOMY IS HEADED TO THE SCANDALS THAT HAVE RECENTLY ROCKED THE MUTUAL FUND INDUSTRY.

I am responsible to my wife and my children, my extended family, my staff and the thousands of clients that we have all over the country that rely on me to make good investment decisions for them. I am also responsible to the hundreds of thousands of listeners who aren't clients but still listen to my words to determine what to do with their money. It's a heavy responsibility, but it does provide its rewards. Clients come to me and say, "Adam, your advice helped me put my kids through college." I have clients who are retiring and managing to meet their personal needs and live a lifestyle they are accustomed to in the worst market in the history of the stock market. There is a lot of satisfaction that comes with that.

That is my story. I have a vision for my business and a set of principles that I am using to enrich the lives of my clients and radio listeners. This book will allow me to fully explore those principals for the benefit of you, my reader. Thank you for tuning in.

CHAPTER TWO

Know Yourself

"HI JEFF. THIS IS ADAM BOLD. WHAT'S
YOUR QUESTION?"

*"Thanks for taking my call, Adam. I
have a quick question and it's
in regards to my 401(k) plan. I'm 28
years old. I've been maxing out my
401(k). I've been doing it for the
past five years and I'm not really
a market timer, but I do take an active
approach in just making sure that
everything is balanced and diversified.
My question is, there's a new program
that my company is offering..."*

KNOW YOURSELF

To thy own self be true. Wise men have reminded us of that basic principle of life for centuries. It should be a guiding light in investing. Before you can put together an investment plan, you really must know what you are trying to accomplish. You need to know your personal limitations—your strengths and weaknesses. There are issues such as risk parameters. How comfortable do you feel with risk? It's not an easy thing to define. Often when you go to a website or talk with an investment adviser or read an article, you will be asked, "Are you a conservative investor, a moderate investor, or an aggressive investor?" In my opinion, those descriptors are too broad and can mean too many different things.

In my mind, risk is a function of volatility. Nobody is happy when their investments go down. However, most people can live with some occasional losses, because they understand that they have to accept some downside in exchange for making money when things go well. Others cannot sleep if they see their account statement and the value is one penny less than they put in. Still others are most troubled when the market goes up 20 percent and their holdings only go up 10 percent. They tell themselves, "Gosh, I should have been more aggressive, so I could have gotten that 20 percent." Or if they lose 10 percent in a market that is down 20 percent. "I can't believe that I lost 10 percent of my money."

Before you develop an investment strategy, you must know more about yourself. Then you can put together a plan that meets your particular needs. How do you begin to discover the type of investor you are? There are questions you can ask yourself. Let's try some. If you received your monthly statement and your account was worth 10 percent less than the month before, what would you do? Would you:

___ Sell everything right away?

___ Be concerned but just continue to monitor your investments?

___ Put in more money because it represents a great opportunity?

Framed this way, the questions challenge you to think about your actions and motivations. It's a

> MOST PEOPLE CAN LIVE WITH LOSSES, BECAUSE THEY UNDERSTAND THAT THEY HAVE TO ACCEPT SOME DOWNSIDE IN EXCHANGE FOR MAKING MONEY WHEN THINGS GO WELL.

much better approach than simply labeling yourself a conservative, moderate or aggressive investor.

KNOWLEDGE IS WORTH GAINING

Knowing yourself is one thing. Knowing your *best* self is quite another. Education comes in to play here. Your current self may not be your best self. You may want to change; you may determine that there is a better self you aspire to become by learning more about investing. The more you learn, the more able you'll be to discern what investment is appropriate for you and what is not.

Also, you must have realistic expectations about achieving your financial goals. One of the things that we probe when we meet with a potential client is what he or she is attempting to accomplish. One client may have a pool of money to supplement her income in retirement. Another client the same age may have money dedicated to pay for college for children currently 6, 8, and 10 years old. With those different time frames and goals, these investors will likely take different paths with risk. Put another way, somebody might take pride in being very conservative, but if all of their money is plopped in very safe investments, they may not be able to amass enough money over time to meet their goals.

SOMEBODY MIGHT TAKE PRIDE IN BEING VERY CONSERVATIVE, BUT IF ALL OF THEIR MONEY IS PLOPPED IN VERY SAFE INVESTMENTS, THEY MAY NOT BE ABLE TO AMASS ENOUGH MONEY OVER TIME TO MEET THEIR GOALS.

Knowing yourself, then acting on it, can be difficult. One big obstacle to self-awareness for most people is inertia. It's always easiest to do nothing. These folks look at the investments they hold and convince themselves that standing still is the safest option. "I know these investments are not as good as they can be, but to change them would be a hassle." It is natural to fear the unknown. You may even own junk investments but are more comfortable with them than with other, better options. Some people are...well, I don't want to say, "lazy." Let's just say they are inattentive. They put their money in Fund A and forget about it. Whether it does poorly or well, they are just not doing much to stay on top of it.

CONSTANT WORRIERS

Then there are those who are so emotional that they make rash decisions that end up costing money. These are the people who panic and sell everything when the market is down for a few days...then jump back in with buckets of cash when the market goes back up. One investor in Las Vegas came to our local The Mutual Fund Store and told us he had been trading stocks on his own at home. He monitored every blip in the stock market on handsome computer monitors. He would sit and watch these monitors, watch CNBC, and the intra-day gyrations

CASE STUDY NO. 3

We were approached by a client who owned 32 different mutual funds held by eight different custodians. Diversification is one of the most important elements in investing and this client had gone out of his way to avoid having too much money in one area. But he was having a hard time managing his funds, was struggling to keep track of what he had, and was looking to get organized.

The client was encountering several problems with all of his funds. Obviously the paperwork and accounting was a nightmare for taxes. Also it was difficult to keep track of how much money he had, how it was performing, and what changes he needed to make. The client believed all this was worthwhile because he was diversifying his investments.

Being this widespread can actually counteract the goal of being diversified. Many of the funds' holdings overlapped and instead of being spread out there was a greater amount of risk than the client believed he had. With too many different funds and custodians it becomes difficult to tell what is working well and what needs to be changed. After reviewing his portfolio he realized it was time to start consolidating his funds and adopt an approach that would be more effective.

CONCLUSION

Diversification is good, but you need to be intelligently diversified. Putting your money in countless different funds will only make it difficult to manage and prevent you from making the best decisions. It is important to have one manager who is setting the direction for your investments and helping you decide what decisions are best for you.

would cause him to feel a need to do something. Over a three-year interval he had very few profitable trades. Finally, he came to us. "I need to have you guys manage this money," he said. One month after opening an account with us, the stock market hit a bad patch and went down every day for a week. Without calling us, our Las Vegas friend on a Friday called Schwab and sold everything in his account. On Monday, the market went up 200 points. He called us again and said, "I made a horrid mistake. I need to get that money back into the market."

This time I had a conversation with him and said we would love to manage his money—but he had to be less impulsive. He agreed. One month later, the market went through another gyration and he once again sold when prices were at their lows. That gentleman knew himself intellectually but emotionally couldn't control himself. Finally, he let go and let us manage his account in the way we thought appropriate. I am not exaggerating when I tell you that he is now one or our happiest clients. Not only because his investment returns improved, but also because of the big emotional burden that has been lifted from his shoulders.

Through the bear market of 2000 to 2002, we had a lot of clients who did very similar things. The terrible part about that bear market was that it lasted three years. Everybody assumed that from time to time things would go down on the way to going up. We went through 2000 and the market was down for a year. Some investors immediately bailed out. Others could make it through one year but after two years of a bear market they sold everything. Some investors after three consecutive bad years told themselves, "The stock market is never going to go back up again," and they jumped out. When the stock market came roaring back in 2003, there were a lot of people who could not benefit from the upturn because they had bailed out of the market. Essentially, they suffered a double whammy—they lost money when the market was down, and lost opportunity when the market went up.

DETACHMENT IS KEY

Certain people do have the emotional capacity to manage their own investments. These investors can separate feelings from intellectual and educated responses. It's OK to feel scared by the market when things pull back. It's OK to feel badly about the market and to be disappointed. However, it is not OK to act rashly on those things. If you are one of those people who cannot separate your emotions from your actions, you probably should hire somebody to make day-to-day investment decisions.

The Bold Truth About Mutual Funds

Admitting to yourself you need help can be difficult. Acknowledging one's mistakes often is harder. Everyone makes mistakes from time to time. The key is to be able to admit when you have made one and to recognize it relatively quickly and move on to something else. Too many people will continue to suffer from their mistakes instead of moving on. Here's how it happens: A broker or adviser recommends an investment to a client, and it goes down in value. The broker will tell his disappointed client, "Just hold on to it. It will come back." Sometimes it will. In many instances, however, the broker is really saying "hold on to this" not because it is a sound investment but because he doesn't want to look stupid to the client by admitting he made a mistake.

At some point you, the wise investor, have to tell yourself—and your advisers—that no matter how good the original idea, the investment is not working...so let's move on to something else.

I have one client, a single parent in her early 40's, who is my cousin. Because of our family connection, I can talk to her a little more frankly than my typical client. Each time we would see each other at holidays she would say, "I really need to come in and have you look at my investments." But inertia prevailed, and she never did. Finally, she came into the office the beginning of 2003 with a relatively small sum of money

IF YOU ARE ONE OF THOSE PEOPLE WHO CANNOT SEPARATE YOUR EMOTIONS FROM YOUR ACTIONS, YOU PROBABLY SHOULD HIRE SOMEBODY TO MAKE DAY-TO-DAY INVESTMENT DECISIONS.

to invest. At the same time, she opened a folder
and pulled out statements for her 401(k) retire-

CASE STUDY NO. 4

*We were approached by a client in her late 40's who had just inherited
a large investment portfolio following her mother's death. The account
was an amalgamation of stocks, which were primarily utilities, and
some mutual funds. These were investments the mother had received
when the father had passed away.*

*For the most part the funds had performed very well over the years, but
the client was concerned about how the money was spread. Most of the
stocks had been acquired by the father during years of work, and the
mother never made any changes to the portfolio because her husband had
always managed the family's finances. These decisions served her parents
well for decades and the client was nervous about making changes.*

*We advised the client to redistribute her finances with a strategy that
would better serve her needs. While the investments served her parents
well, the economic climate had changed and she had different needs
and goals. While these funds had done very well in the past they were
not the type of investments we would recommend for someone in this
particular client's position.*

CONCLUSION

*Inherited stocks and securities should be treated as if they were in cash.
Take the holdings and start with a clean slate, investing the money in
a manner that is best suited for your needs. In essence you are being
given the chance to make a fresh investment and start a whole new
portfolio. Instead of allowing someone else to make your decisions, find
a plan that works for you.*

ment account—which was fully invested in money market funds. I immediately told her she needed to put a good portion of the funds into other investments and sketched out a variety of places that would make sense and provide her with a balanced portfolio. One year later, we sat down to have a year-end review. I showed her the performance of her account, where we had invested in mutual funds. It did very well, growing 35 percent. I asked about her 401(k). Despite my recommendations, she never moved a dime of her funds out of the money market funds. "At least I didn't lose any money," she sheepishly said. I quickly did some calculations. I then informed her that had she invested her 401(k) funds in the variety of mutual funds one year earlier, as I had suggested, she would have made a profit of $35,000 instead of $3,000. I watched her face and I could see the proverbial light go on in her head. She finally realized that her fear of losing money was actually costing her money, and that could very well mean that she would not have adequate financial resources to retire.

LIVING IN THE PAST...NOT!

Here's another personality type. I meet a lot of people of retirement age. All of their life they've saved money. They have accumulated considerable wealth. When they prepare to retire, they find it very difficult to spend their money. They feel a need to make sure their money keeps accumulating. I tell those people, "Look, the reason that you accumulated this money was so that you could ultimately spend it—now. If your portfolio is generating more money than you spend, then ultimately all you're going to do is leave a bigger estate for your kids." One of my philosophies is that whether you leave $50,000, $500,000 or $5 million to your children, they should be appreciative. That's money that you earned, not money that they earned. If you can enjoy your life more, you should do that. People should take more vacations and do what they enjoy most, because that is the reason they worked hard to accumulate a nest egg. When people retire, they have to change their mind set. It is not easy.

While some are too cautious, others do not exercise sufficient self-restraint. I deal with a lot of entrepreneurs who are natural risk takers. They are comfortable with the volatility of the market and, indeed, thrive on it. Some get to a point where they've been successful over the years and have accumulated large amounts of money. They will come to me and say they want to be very aggressive and "swing for the fences." It's difficult to get such people to re-assess their attitudes. Here's what I try to tell them:

The Bold Truth About Mutual Funds

"Right now, you're earning $x per year. Now with this money that you've accumulated, if we get a 3 percent rate-of-return we can generate the same amount of income with you not working as you make when you're working. There's no reason to take 'swing-for-the-fences' risk, when you don't need to. You don't need a 40 percent return to maintain your lifestyle."

I KNOW MYSELF

Know yourself. I know myself. When I was picking stocks, I was a sucker for a "good story" and I therefore was not very good at picking stocks. So I've decided I'm not going to buy individual stocks. On the other hand, I've learned that I'm good at picking mutual funds, and that has been a key to my building my personal wealth. I own the very same funds I recommend for our clients.

Once you have done the hard work of introspection, the next step—turning to experts to help you achieve your objectives—may seem easy. However, it is not. Who you turn to has huge implications for the outcome of your investment planning. Take great care in picking your advisers, because it will ultimately pay vast dividends.

CHAPTER THREE

Selecting a
Broker or Adviser

"RICHARD, YOU'RE ON THE AIR. THIS IS
ADAM BOLD. HOW CAN I HELP YOU?"

*"Our broker suggested a fund
to us called the Hartford Leaders,
a tax-deferred variable
annuity. We were wondering
about that. This is regular money.
I am 79 and my wife is 74."*

SELECTING A BROKER OR ADVISER

Maybe you have decided that you are not the best person to develop and implement a multifaceted investment strategy to best nurture your personal investments. There is no shame there. It is no admission of personal weakness or failure. It does not reflect on the soundness of your education. You are not flawed. Your children and dog will not hate you. Perhaps you recognize that you could educate yourself to be a smart investor, but prefer not to because you would rather spend time with your family, work at your career—or go fishing. Other priorities reign in your life.

You also are convinced that investments are too important to be locked in a drawer and forgotten. A strategy must be developed and then executed over time. You therefore set out to recruit someone in the best position to provide sound, rewarding investment advice on an ongoing basis. There are armies of candidates eager for the assignment.

Yet it is surprising that many of us do not give much thought to how to evaluate the hoards of financial planners, stock brokers and others eager to tell us where THEY would like to put YOUR money, if only given the chance.

Frequently, we inherit advisers we never evaluated. Here's a quick test. Jot down all the investment retirement accounts you have opened with employers you have worked for over the years; all the mutual fund accounts you have set up; all the brokerage accounts you hold. Have you ever met face-to face the investment advisers listed on your quarterly statement? There is a good chance that you haven't. Odds are that if you ever did, that person is no longer working for the firm, and the name listed as your representative "inherited" your account. You would never turn the proceeds of your paycheck over to someone you do not know. Yet chances are that you, like most everyone, are willing to leave the funds you set aside for your twilight years, your children's education and your future well-being in the hands of a total stranger.

If you take nothing else from the book you now hold in your hands, be resolved that you will never again blissfully entrust your personal riches to anyone you do not know. You *will* interview him or her. And when you do, ask one of the most important questions: How are they compensated? Simply put, are they providing

IF YOU TAKE NOTHING ELSE FROM THE BOOK YOU NOW HOLD IN YOUR HANDS, BE RESOLVED THAT YOU WILL NEVER AGAIN BLISSFULLY ENTRUST YOUR PERSONAL RICHES TO ANYONE YOU DO NOT KNOW.

advice to you or are they selling products—thus benefiting a third party but perhaps not yourself?

DO THEY KNOW YOU?

Every adviser is required to know their client. That is a U.S. Securities and Exchange Commission (SEC) regulation; the rule is titled the "Know your client rule." Advisers are supposed to determine investors' time horizons, their risk tolerances and their goals and aspirations. However, advisers are often in a hurry, or they have their own philosophies and expectations that they indirectly force on their client. Often they don't listen to a client as much as they should.

Consider the origins of your relationship with an adviser or broker. If you are fortunate and have $10 million to invest, you can go to Goldman Sachs or a private bank such as Bank of America and advisers in pinstripe suits will gladly manage your money for a fee. Most people working with a more modest nest egg, however, end up working with a retail broker who receives commissions rather than a fee. And not all brokers are alike. If you call Merrill Lynch and say, "I need to talk to a broker," you will in most instances be routed to a trainee broker who does not have a full roster of clients.

The Bold Truth About Mutual Funds

How does that broker operate? During my
stint at Smith Barney, the firm had research
analysts who provided coverage on about 400
stocks. Of those 400 stocks, about 250 were either
buy- or hold-rated. There were only three stocks
rated as a "sell!" As a Smith Barney broker sitting
in Kansas City, I had to pick from those "highly
rated" 250 stocks and figure out which ones to sell
to my clients. What they taught me in training
was to sell the securities that had the best stories.
When I called a client to get them to do a transaction, I had to come up with a convincing story. I
remember recommending the stock of a biotech-
nology company founded by Jonas Salk, the devel-
oper of the polio vaccine. With Salk, I had a great
story to tell. I didn't need to get bogged down
with my client in a detailed discussion about the
financial fundamentals of the company.

> **WHAT THEY TAUGHT ME IN TRAINING WAS TO SELL THE SECURITIES THAT HAD THE BEST STORIES. WHEN I CALLED A CLIENT TO GET THEM TO DO A TRANSACTION, I HAD TO COME UP WITH A GOOD STORY.**

If you want to be a smart investor in stocks,
though, you have to be able to tell the difference
between a good story and a good stock.
Furthermore, you have to be able to separate
what is a good company from what is a good
stock, and you have to know when to buy and
when to sell. Your emotions may cause you to
shun the sound enterprise and favor a hot stock.
A lot of good companies produce poor stocks,
and a lot of bad companies turn out good stocks.

Finding the right stock can be vexing—
particularly for those who do not know where to

look. Consider this: Fully 80 percent of mutual fund managers—the guys who have access to all the Byzantine research and the most powerful computers—under-perform the market. Amazing. And why? Here is a little secret: Investment performance is not always their top concern. Back when I was a broker, we had these "squawk boxes"—little speakers—on our desk. All of a sudden, they would come to life and a remote voice would intone, "We have 10,000 shares of Stock X in our inventory and if you sell shares to our clients we will pay you an extra 50 cents-per-share commission." The client, of course, was clueless about all this. So I'm sitting there thinking that if Smith Barney didn't want Stock X in its inventory, why would my client want it in theirs?

INFORMATION IS POWER

Times, however, are changing—to the potential benefit of consumers and small investors. Information is empowering us in all areas of endeavor. For instance, there was a time—and it was not long ago—when car dealers knew how much they paid for a car and you didn't. Now with the Internet, you can find exactly what the car dealer paid. When you negotiate with him, you have a better idea of what's a fair deal. In this age of information, people have just begun to take advantage of the information at

The Bold Truth About Mutual Funds

their disposal. This information revolution is already reforming investment markets.

Recently, major scandals have broken out on Wall Street after it was disclosed that respected brokerages such as Merrill Lynch were publishing research reports saying that a stock was a "buy" while privately the analyst would tell co-workers that the stock was junk and should be sold. As investors start to learn of such practices, they realize they need to ask more questions. And again, the primary question to ask a potential adviser is how he or she wishes to be compensated. When somebody says, "I am compensated every time I sell something to you," you need to say, "Well, thank you very much, but I need to find somebody else."

> **WHEN SOMEBODY SAYS, "I AM COMPENSATED EVERY TIME I SELL SOMETHING TO YOU," YOU NEED TO SAY, "WELL, THANK YOU VERY MUCH, BUT I NEED TO FIND SOMEBODY ELSE."**

Why? On top of evaluating the merits of the investment, every time he makes a recommendation you are forced to wonder if he is recommending a product because it's good for you or because he needs to boost his income. When I worked for Smith Barney, if I could get you to buy something I'd get paid. If I could get you to sell it, I'd get paid again. If I could get you to buy something else with the proceeds, I'd get paid again. If you made a wise investment and kept if for the next 10 years I *never* got paid again. Talk about a situation ripe for conflict of interest!

This problem also applies to mutual funds. Consider funds that carry upfront fees paid at the

FINDING THE RIGHT INVESTMENT ADVISER: SOME TIPS

Once you decide you need help in managing your investments, how do you go about finding the right adviser? Choosing the right one can be just as tough as putting together the right investment plan.

The first factor to determine is how the adviser is compensated. Typically there are three ways. First, some work on a "transactional" basis. This means the adviser gets paid a commission each time he gets you to buy or sell something inside your account, including load mutual funds.

This method is inherently unfair to both you and the broker. When you go to someone to help with your investments, you are seeking objective advice. Instead, the transactional adviser is not paid for giving advice; he is paid for buying and selling investments.

As a practical matter, such advisers don't have much incentive to monitor the investments going forward. Whether the investments do well or poorly, he still gets his fees up front. Plus, the commissioned broker is always like a lion searching for his next meal. In order to get paid he constantly must search for the next customer. This doesn't leave him much time to look after the investments he has sold in the past.

The second form of compensation is "fee basis." This means the adviser gets paid a percentage of the value of the accounts he is managing for you. I believe this is the fairest method of payment, for a number of reasons. First, there are no incentives for the adviser to do transactions just to generate revenues. Whether he does one transaction a year or a thousand, he gets paid exactly the same.

Second, the adviser's interests are aligned with yours. The only way he can make more money is if your portfolio grows. In other words, if the adviser doubles the size of your accounts, you will pay him twice as much. You will be happy because you will have more money; he will be happy because he is getting paid more.

Last, when you pay on a fee basis, you are free to leave at any time and take your accounts elsewhere. This puts pressure on the adviser to watch your account to make sure your investments are always in the right things.

The third form of compensation is an hourly rate - typically done by financial planners who prepare a one-time financial plan. You get the product the adviser promised, but you do not get ongoing oversight. When you need reviews you will have to pay additional fees. Some advisers charge an hourly fee for their initial work, and then sell commission-based products to implement the plan.

It is also important that you discuss your expectations of service with the adviser. How often can you expect to hear from them? I believe, at minimum, you should hear from your adviser at least twice per year. The adviser should use these conversations as an opportunity to fill you in on his current market outlook, the status of your investments, and to ask if anything has changed in your personal situation which would affect the way your accounts are allocated.

One of the comments I hear most frequently from callers to my radio show is something like, "He sold me a fund three years ago, and I haven't heard from him since." The way I see it, when an adviser agrees to take money in exchange for investment advice, he owes it to the client to stay in regular communication.

As I said, two calls should be the minimum. At my company, The Mutual Fund Store, we have a computerized system that provides each of my investment advisers with a list of all the clients they need to contact each month. This automated system ensures that every client is called at least twice per year.

Another very important expectation is that the adviser admits when he has made a mistake. There are an awful lot of advisers who are afraid to admit they goofed, because it might make them look stupid.

Last, I think you should expect periodic performance reporting from your adviser. All investment custodians are required to send regular statements to their clients. These statements, however, typically just show the total value of the account, the investments held, and a recap of any transactions that were done in the last period. Not necessarily performance.

time of purchase. The broker sells you these funds and he gets his commission upfront. So, this week, he gets a paycheck. But next week, if he wants a paycheck, he has to find somebody else to ring up a sale and register a commission. Because there are only so many hours in a week, over time he'll be too busy searching for new clients and not much interested in following up with you. Clearly he's a salesman...not an adviser.

There is an insidious side to these commissions. Consider the math of a "load fund"—that is, a mutual fund that generates a commission charge. The client loses out on the "load" (the commission paid) and he also loses out on the compounding growth on the load. If a client invests $10,000 and there is a 5 percent commission, then only $9,500 actually gets invested. The investment has to climb from $9,500 to $10,000 just to get the investor back to where he started. The good news is that there are many, many no-load mutual funds. It's foolish to invest in a load fund. If there were two gas stations that each charged $1.50 a gallon for gas, but one charged an extra $20 just to put the pump into your car, would anyone ever go to that gas station?

So steer clear of those who advocate mutual funds that carry a load. Furthermore, steer clear of those who work for a particular mutual fund company and push the company's products. Those who work for Waddell & Reed, for example,

> **THERE IS AN INSIDIOUS SIDE TO THESE COMMISSIONS. CONSIDER THE MATH OF A "LOAD FUND"— THAT IS, A MUTUAL FUND THAT GENERATES A COMMISSION CHARGE.**

primarily sell Waddell & Reed funds. Anytime you're approached by such representatives, ask yourself: "Are they recommending this to me because it's good for me, or are they recommending this because it's good for their company?"

In all likelihood, they are not searching from the entire universe of investments to find the very best ones for you. The average person should have a portfolio containing seven to a dozen different mutual funds. What are the odds that the 10 best mutual funds in the world are from one family of mutual funds? Pretty slim.

There also are mutual fund wholesalers who work for specific mutual fund companies. Their job is to get brokers and financial advisers to sell their funds instead of those from other companies. A wholesaler will go to a branch office at a brokerage house and host a luncheon. Many of the brokers will come to get the free meal. The question that the brokers in the office most often ask is not, "Who is here and what are they going to be talking about?" Rather, they ask, "What's for lunch?"

These brokers are not evil. They aren't trying to do the wrong thing, but the system is set up in such a way that in order for them to be successful they have to think about themselves first, rather than you the client.

There are a variety of ways that mutual fund companies or brokerage houses motivate their

> THE AVERAGE PERSON SHOULD HAVE A PORTFOLIO CONTAINING SEVEN TO A DOZEN DIFFERENT MUTUAL FUNDS. WHAT ARE THE ODDS THAT THE 10 BEST MUTUAL FUNDS IN THE WORLD ARE FROM ONE FAMILY OF MUTUAL FUNDS? PRETTY SLIM.

staff to sell certain products. Let's look at the "preferred fund lists" that various brokerages maintain. Edward Jones, for example, had a preferred fund list that it would tout to clients. As a client, you probably would think that a fund makes the list because of superior performance. However, the reality is that a fund would get on that list when the fund company paid Edward Jones perhaps $500,000 to $1 million, plus 30 percent of their ongoing management expenses. Edward Jones brokers aren't restricted from selling funds not on the list. It turns out, though, that in 2002 85 percent of Edward Jones's sales were funds on the preferred list. A remarkable coincidence? I think not. Jones paid a $75 million fine for engaging in this practice.

IT'S YOUR JOB

That brings us back to your responsibilities as a smart investor. Interview your potential adviser! Ask them about their experience level, how long they have provided investment advice and also what professional designations they have earned. For example, in my case I have two designations. I have a CMFC, which is a Chartered Mutual Fund Counselor earned from The College for Financial Planning in Boulder, Colorado, and I also have a CFS, Certified Funds

Specialist, designation, that I earned from the Institute for Business and Finance in LaJolla, California. What do those two things mean? I have had advanced training in the area of mutual funds. Now, if somebody was looking for a broker or an adviser to help them trade stocks, I don't think I would be the right guy. Those who have earned the CFP, or Certified Financial Planner, designation are trained to offer a broad spectrum of investment management, estate planning, insurance and tax advice. If you are looking for a generalist, a CFP may be perfect for you. If you are looking for just an investment manager, the CFP is good but not essential.

These designations and distinctions have value. They signal that a person has a commitment to his or her profession and to the specific parts of the business that are their main focus of attention.

Unfortunately, sometimes the service offerings get muddled. Increasingly, there are independent practices and accounting firms that now offer investment advice. My approach has been to do this one thing—investment management. It takes 100 percent of my time and effort to be the best at what I do. If people want insurance, and people do need insurance, we refer them to someone else. If they need tax planning, I will refer them to an accountant. While I might be able to make more money selling those other services, it would dilute my ability to be the very best at the things that I do.

Your efforts to proactively monitor and oversee your investments do not end once you have found a highly competent adviser, ascertained how he or she is paid and entered into a relationship. With your new partner, you must thoughtfully and deliberately devise and implement a robust, rational plan.

CHAPTER FOUR

Have a Plan

"LET'S GO TO STEVE. HI STEVE,
YOU'RE ON THE AIR. WHAT'S YOUR
QUESTION TODAY?"

*"I've got a family of five with three kids
and we're trying to do some college
planning and interested in the 529 college
plan but more specifically than just the
plan itself. I am from Indiana and Indiana
gives no incentive to invest in their plan,
let alone any advantage from a tax standpoint.
Secondly, my concern is the kids are
9, 8 and 7. With the length of time that I
have to invest, don't I have a pretty
good possibility of the government
changing the rules on the investment?
Am I better off investing myself?"*

HAVE A PLAN

Great accomplishments almost always require a plan. If you are going to build a bridge, you don't just start building and hope that it can support what it needs to hold up, especially in hurricane winds and during periods of great stress. If you have to go in today and have your appendix out, the surgeon will have a plan. If something unexpected arises, he will deal with it and then go back to completing the plan. The same thing is true with your investments; you must have an all encompassing plan, a strategy, an evolving blueprint.

Most investors, however, have no inkling of a plan. Typically, they make many uncoordinated efforts to accumulate investments over a period of time. That's just not good enough—particularly in today's high-risk, fast-changing world.

For example, a person might see an article in a magazine about a stellar-performing mutual fund. He or she pulls $10,000 from a checking account and rushes to buy $10,000 of that mutual fund. Then a few months later a broker will call with an exclusive tip (that he and dozens of other brokers are pushing to hundreds of clients). The individual now takes $5,000 from the checking account and buys $5,000 worth of shares in that stock. The question is, why did the investor put $10,000 in the mutual fund and $5,000 in the stock? Was it a strategic decision? No. It was an unplanned response. Over a period of time most investors—way too many investors—make a variety of investments and they end up with pools of money all over the place. They have no cohesive strategy.

Keep in mind the following when constructing your plan:

○ What's the end-goal of your investment? Retirement income? College funding?

○ Asset allocation is essential. Mixing it up is a good thing!

○ Always…always…keep an eye on risk and your current circumstances.

○ Please, don't be a fickle investor. Discipline is key.

○ And don't just plan once. You need to plan again…and again.

> OVER A PERIOD OF TIME MOST INVESTORS— WAY TOO MANY INVESTORS— MAKE A VARIETY OF INVESTMENTS AND THEY END UP WITH POOLS OF MONEY ALL OVER THE PLACE. THEY HAVE NO COHESIVE STRATEGY.

WHAT'S YOUR GOAL?

In order to build a plan you have to know your overarching personal goal. You don't necessarily have to define your goal with great precision. The farther out the goal is, the less specific it needs to be. In other words, when somebody is 30 years old, a reasonable goal is to accumulate money for retirement. You cannot—with any precision—put together a specific plan for generating $4,000 a month of investment income 35 years from now. There are too many variables, and you would have to make too many assumptions. However, we can make some limited assumptions and deploy reasonable strategies—and then make adjustments along the way.

While you may not be able to be too precise in delineating your goals, the discipline of identifying and focusing on goals is an invaluable step toward achieving your financial objectives. Do not be vague or imprecise. It serves no purpose to say that you are "out to maximize wealth." What is considered wealth to one person may seem excessive—or paltry—to others. So strive for a balanced approach to goal setting; we must avoid being too precise or too general.

Once identified, your goal dictates an action plan. If your aim is to pay for your children's college education, then you can put together a plan so that you accumulate the necessary money.

Goal-setting requires you to define your time

horizon. If somebody is 35 years away from retirement, my advice to that person is, "Save as much as you can!" If you are 10 to 15 years away from retirement, then we need to look at very specific income numbers. Is the income you feel you'll need at that time even feasible, or do you need to save more each month?

Let's consider a hypothetical situation in some detail. Say your goal 15 years from now is to have income of $5,000 per month. We can project how much your Social Security benefits will be. Let's say it is $1,200 a month. So now we know you need to come up with another $3,800 a month. In order to make that work, we might conclude that you will need to accumulate investments amounting to $700,000 in 15 years. That triggers a whole new set of determinations: In coming years, how is that money going to be invested and at what rate of return? We also have to make some assumptions about inflation. To what extent is your buying power going to erode? And when you start drawing income from the savings, will it come from interest and dividends on the investments, or will you be taking out principal as well? In short, will the $700,000 be enough, and if not, how much more money will you need to contribute each month to your investment portfolio? Now we are getting closer to establishing a plan, a blueprint for ultimately achieving $5,000 dollars a month in income.

A married couple wants to save money for their three young children to go to college and wants to know what investments are best suited to their needs. The family's first thought was to start Coverdale IRA's (formerly known as Educational IRA's). There were two primary concerns for using a Coverdale IRA for this family, the first of which was the income restriction. Both parents held jobs and it was conceivable they would reach a point where the annual household income would exclude them from the benefits of a Coverdale IRA. Additionally, while the couple's youngest child still had several years before he would need the money, the oldest child was due to start college in the not too distant future. The limits on annual contributions would have prevented the family from committing as much money to the fund as they would have liked.

The family also discussed setting up Uniform Gift to Minor accounts. The concern with that approach is once the child reaches the age of majority (18 or 21, depending on the state) the money becomes theirs by law and the parents have no control over how it is spent. The family had no particular reason to be concerned about any of their children misusing the accounts but they still had reservations about handing over a large sum of money to a teenager.

The couple had also investigated the state-sponsored 529 plans available. They were very attracted to the tax benefits of the plan and felt comfortable with the general structure. The one major concern about 529 plans is that they are run by elected officials. So they tend to be extremely conservative, and it is rare for a 529 to show a strong return. No official wants to be associated with an education plan that loses money so they go about structuring a plan to avoid losing money instead of focusing on ways to generate a strong investment return.

Also, the investment options are limited and the restrictions on making changes are very tight.

CONCLUSION

The final decision the couple made was to start a new investment fund jointly held by the two of them. It was understood that the money in this account was only to be used for college expenses for the three children. This offered them the flexibility to manage the account as they saw best and also offered them more options on how to use the money when the time came to pay for college. This plan assured the couple the best way to save enough money to offer each of their children an equal opportunity at a college education. On the surface there appears to be many benefits to the various college investment funds but the reality is the restrictions on these plans outweigh the benefits. To a smart investor the best approach is to make intelligent, responsible decisions and avoid limiting your options.

ASSET ALLOCATION IS KEY

The investment universe, however, is dynamic and constantly changing. A good investment advisor works closely with a client to put together a plan today. Part of that process includes an asset allocation plan. The term "asset allocation plan" means how your money should be split up between different types of investments. As time goes by and market conditions change, you'll need to make changes to the allocation plan.

At any one time, the advisers at my firm have a group of about 14 investment models I have developed to use as templates for different types of clients. Typically, our portfolios have somewhere between seven and 10 different kinds of investments. There are 28 different asset classes that we choose from when we set up an individual portfolio including money market-funds, international stocks, international bonds, large capitalization stocks, small-cap stocks, growth stocks and value stocks and so forth. My job is to find the best fund in each of the seven to 10 asset classes identified for a client. The asset allocation tells us what kind of funds to own. The issue then becomes which ones.

It is also important to rebalance from time to time. Say a client starts with 50 percent in stocks and 50 percent in bonds. Over time, he might end up with 70 percent of his portfolio value tied up in stocks because of a general market rise. By rebalancing, you will be taking some profits from things that have run up, and be putting money into things that have not gone up as much—and perhaps represent a better value now.

When this happens, many clients say they don't want to sell shares to rebalance their portfolio because it will generate a tax hit. That is

THE TERM "ASSET ALLOCATION PLAN" MEANS HOW YOUR MONEY SHOULD BE SPLIT UP BETWEEN DIFFERENT TYPES OF INVESTMENTS. AS TIME GOES BY AND MARKET CONDITIONS CHANGE, YOU'LL NEED TO MAKE CHANGES TO THE ALLOCATION PLAN.

faulty logic. Of course, we always try to minimize the impact of taxes on clients. Thus, we may have one plan for taxable investments and another for tax-deferred investments. But, taxes are never a reason not to sell something that should be sold.

ALWAYS MONITOR RISK

As you come close to achieving your goal, you also need to reassess risk. Say that your objective is that in 15 years you will have $1 million. As you get three or four years away from reaching that $1 million target, you probably want to have a portfolio that's going to have less volatility so that you don't risk losing the handsome nest egg you have worked so hard to accumulate.

No matter what your goal may be, my experience has convinced me that mutual funds are the investment vehicle of choice. My core philosophy is that if you are going to take the risk of the market, you owe it to yourself to be in the best investments possible. Whether you own a good fund or bad fund, there is market risk. If the stock market goes down, both the bad fund and the good fund go down in value. The difference is that in good markets a good fund goes up more than a bad fund. And in a bad market, the good fund declines less in value than a poor fund. If we can make more in the good times and lose less in the bad times, the average returns will be very good. This represents a consistency of performance that should be treasured. The same thing holds true for bond funds. There are a lot of funds out there that have similar risk parameters, but there are some managers who are consistently just better performers than others.

Unfortunately, the vast majority of people calling themselves investment counselors never really take the time to help clients craft an investment plan—or identify the best funds to utilize. They sell investments. If the adviser gets a fee upfront for selling you an investment, he is supposed to assume a fiduciary responsibility to continue to monitor your investments—forever. As things change, as your plan needs to be adapted to changing times, market conditions or changing events in your life, he is supposed to talk with you periodically. He is supposed to tell you, "I think we need to do something different and here's why." But, unfortunately, an awful lot of brokers abdicate these responsibilities.

DON'T BE A FICKLE INVESTOR

Of course, the adviser is not always the one to blame. Too often, the investor unwittingly throws up barriers to achieving his financial objectives. As time goes by, some investors let their emotions steer them from their plan. For example, an investor determines that to achieve a goal she needs to save and invest $1,000 a month. Every month, $1,000 gets invested into her 401(k) retirement account or mutual funds. Then a year comes along like 2000 and the market goes down. The investor tells herself, "I put $12,000 into this thing in 2000 and now it's worth $10,000 dollars. I can live with that." Then along comes 2001 and her initial $12,000 investment is worth $9,000. So the investor tells herself, "I'm not doing this any more. I'm not going to pour more money into a losing proposition." So she liquidates her holdings just before the market registers a significant rebound.

Some people have horrible timing. They will buy when stock valuations are at an all time high and sell when stocks probe record lows. These people let emotions rule. I have some clients who put together a plan and are doing great but they can't just sit back and watch it grow. They have to do something. They will call me up and say, "We own the XYZ fund and it made 24 percent last year in a market that was up 20 percent. But we have found a fund that was up 29 percent, so let's move our money into this new fund." I will point out that the fund they currently hold has out-performed the market for several consecutive years—and they should stay with it. They don't

SOME PEOPLE HAVE HORRIBLE TIMING. THEY WILL BUY WHEN STOCK VALUATIONS ARE AT AN ALL TIME HIGH AND SELL WHEN STOCKS PROBE RECORD LOWS. THESE PEOPLE LET EMOTIONS RULE.

care. Some people are tinkerers. A lot of times you hurt yourself by doing that…because you abandon your plan!

The 2000-2002 bear market was bad news for people who already had built up a significant nest egg—only to watch it decline in value. However, investors who continue to accumulate investments in bad times as well as good times are ultimately rewarded. They accumulate more shares for a lesser price than those who buy only when the market is up.

PLAN ONCE… AND PLAN AGAIN!

Investors need to sit down every six months to a year and assess which of their investments have done well and which have performed poorly. If they are working with an adviser, the adviser should do this for them. The question I ask myself when I look at client accounts is simple but significant: "Is there anything that we can own today that is better than what we already own?" Many investors have a hard time realizing the wisdom of taking profits when it is appropriate.

It is also important to adjust your investments to stick to your plan. Perhaps in 1996 you started out with a portfolio that was 50 percent stocks and 50 percent bonds. By the end of 1999,

C A S E   S T U D Y   N O.   6

Sometimes the amount of money available to invest changes suddenly. One client had been watching a piece of real estate appreciate for several years and finally chose to sell it at a substantial profit. Now he was looking for direction on how to invest the sizeable amount of cash he had. He decided to put the money into mutual funds and stocks as opposed to re-investing in real estate but was unsure about how much to invest at one time.

The major factor in this decision is timing. If the market is particularly high it is wise to exercise some restraint and invest a smaller portion of the money. On the other hand, if the market is low and there are undervalued opportunities available it makes sense to move quicker and put more of the money in immediately. With those factors in mind the following is a solid plan offering the benefits of both situations:

Invest 50 percent of the money immediately and hold onto the rest with a defined, structured formula for how and when you will put it into the market. This way if stocks start going up the day after you invest you are participating, and if prices slide after your initial entrance you still have funds to buy in at the lower rate. Whatever happens, it is vital that you stick with the schedule you have drawn up.

CONCLUSION

It is important to have strategic plans and stick to them. Once you decide how to invest the money, you have to be faithful to your plan. It is very easy to fall into a trap where you see prices start to slip and you become afraid to invest, or if stocks go up you hesitate and wait for the prices to come back down. Once you develop a plan, you need to stick with it. See next chapter.

the portfolio may have been 80 percent stocks and 20 percent bonds. If you didn't do anything, you were slammed by the bear market of 2000, 2001 and 2002. After the stock declines and the bull market for bonds, your entire "pie" would have shrunk and your portfolio might have been 70 percent bonds and 30 percent stocks.

On the other hand, if you and your adviser regularly rebalanced your portfolio to maintain 50 percent stocks and 50 percent bonds, the impact of the bear market would have been reduced and your average return over time would have been quite excellent. Perhaps you wouldn't have made quite as much money in the good years, because in 1996 the market went up a lot. (Logic tells you there is no way to know in advance how things are going to work out.) However, I am convinced that if you stick to your plan and you periodically rebalance and periodically reevaluate, you will win over time.

Furthermore, you need to have exposure to a lot of different kinds of investments at all times. Sometimes we are going to miss out on maximizing every last drop of returns out of a particular portfolio. What I am describing is consistency of performance. The best way to build great wealth is with consistent performance.

Our clients give us the authority to change their portfolio on a "discretionary" basis. That is, without calling to ask first. They are paying us for our advice and they know they need to let us do what we need to do to maximize the return on their investment. Those who work on a commission basis cannot ethically manage money on a discretionary basis. You would have to question their motives every time they bought or sold something. Are they doing it because it is right for you as the client or because it generates more fees? I believe investors should totally shun transaction fees. Advisers who use a fee structure like ours get paid exactly the same whether they execute one transaction or 100.

Throughout all our activities on behalf of our clients, however, we are diligently mindful of the plans that they and we have collaboratively crafted and adapted over the years. Those plans provide the compass we use to arrange their investment holdings in the most rational, productive manner we know.

Ultimately, it is your responsibility to carefully plan for the future and engage professionals who can help you refine and execute your plan.

THOSE WHO WORK ON A COMMISSION BASIS CANNOT ETHICALLY MANAGE MONEY ON A DISCRETIONARY BASIS. YOU HAVE TO QUESTION THEIR MOTIVES EVERY TIME THEY BOUGHT OR SOLD SOMETHING.

CHAPTER FIVE

Fine-tuning Your Plan

"HI, RON. WELCOME TO THE SHOW.
WHAT'S YOUR QUESTION?"

*"I am somewhat of a layman as far
as funding goes and I am eligible now,
in the business that I work at, to put
in for my 401(k) and such. But it's
going to be a limited amount because
we are a single-income household
and so I'm not going to be able to put in
that much. Would it be more beneficial
to me to focus in one particular
area of funds rather than trying
to spread it out, since it will be a
smaller amount of money?"*

FINE-TUNING YOUR PLAN

Over my many years of guiding investment clients and studying investor behavior, I have found over and over that I was asserting 10 broad principles. They have helped guide the beginning investor as well as reinforced the best instincts of more savvy market players. Some are "do's." Others are "do not's." There is no clearer, more forceful way of stressing the importance of these foundation principles than presenting them as my 10 Commandments of Investing.

Six of these principles have already been introduced and elaborated upon in earlier chapters. Like the 10 Commandments of the Bible, they are simple, powerful principles to live by. Once accepted, they become self-evident in their logic. They are:

1. YOU SHALL KNOW THYSELF!

2. YOU SHALL KNOW THY ADVISER!

3. YOU SHALL HAVE A PLAN!

4. YOU SHALL BE IN THE BEST
   FUNDS POSSIBLE!

5. YOU SHALL NOT PAY A
   LOAD!

6. YOU SHALL STICK TO YOUR
   PLAN! (DON'T LET EMO-
   TIONS RULE!)

In this chapter, we will explore four
remaining principles that complete our Investor's
Decalogue. Collectively, they round out a complete set of strategies for remaining loyal to the
spirit and letter of the investment plan that
you have devised under the tutelage of a trusted
investment counselor. Some are narrower than
others, but I have elevated them to commandments because they are essential to your
achieving your goals.

The remaining principles:

7. YOU SHALL SAVE!

8. YOU SHALL BE PROACTIVE
   WITH YOUR 401(K)!

9. YOU SHALL NOT BUY WHAT
   YOU DON'T UNDERSTAND!

10. YOU SHALL SHUN
ANNUITIES!

And a concluding overarching credo to live by,
an 11th Commandment, if you will:

o LIVE WELL FOR YOU CANNOT
TAKE IT WITH YOU!

THE IMPORTANCE OF SAVING

I CONTEND
THAT IF YOU
WAIT UNTIL YOU
GET A LARGE
SUM OF MONEY
TOGETHER
YOU'LL NEVER
GET THERE,
BECAUSE IF THE
MONEY IS IN
YOUR CHECKING
ACCOUNT
YOU WILL LIKELY
SPEND IT.

It is hard for people to develop the discipline of regularly saving.

The key to building wealth is to encourage investors to develop the discipline of saving and investing. I talk to a lot of people. Young people, people just starting their careers, often will say, "I'm going to wait until I get $10,000 and then I am going to invest it." I contend that if you wait until you get a large sum of money together you'll never get there, because if the money is in your checking account you will likely spend it.

Go ahead and start investing. Now is the best time. Any amount is sufficient. That is my advice. Start with a single mutual fund. For example, one of the funds that I recommend is the Excelsior Value and Restructuring Fund. They'll let you start an account with a mere $250 and they'll let you add as little as $50 at a time. You can start an automatic investment plan where every month, on the same date, they will take $50 out of your checking account and they will add it to your account at the mutual fund. If you have $50 or $100 in your checking account, it will get spent. Count on it. You'll go out to dinner or you will go get some clothes. If that money has already been taken out of your account, your lifestyle is likely not going to be affected. If you can save $100 a month, then after a year you'll have $1,200 in the account—and perhaps even more, assuming your investment grows in value. After two years you'll have at least $2,400. Soon you will look at your account and be surprised to see you have $5,000. As time goes by, you won't even notice the $100 a month coming out of your checking account; you will just get used to it. When you get a raise, increase your monthly contribution from $100 to $200 a month. Over a period of time, just raise the amounts that you are putting in. Your savings will build up very quickly

PAY OFF DEBT

For most would-be investors, however, getting into a regular habit of saving first requires managing and eliminating personal debt acquired over the years.

There is good debt, bad debt and there is reasonable debt. Mortgage interest is good debt. When I die, I will have a mortgage. I will likely never fully pay it off because mortgage debt is good debt. People—mistakenly, I believe—are in a big hurry to pay off their home. People have an innate belief that if you own "the farm" the bank can't take it away. But we don't live in the Depression Era; we live in a very different world. I bought a new house in 2003 and was able to get a 5 ½ percent mortgage and the interest I pay on it is tax deductible. So I save, right off the top, roughly one-third of my interest payments in the form of lower taxes. One-third of 5.5 percent is roughly 1.8 percent. So my net cost of funds is about 3.7 percent. Now the question is, can I take the money that I would otherwise use to pay down my mortgage and earn more than 3.7 percent a year on it? Every dollar that I earn at over 3.7 percent is an incremental dollar that I will someday have available to me for retirement or for other uses. Thus, mortgage debt is good debt; it makes sense to carry that debt. It doesn't mean that people who have lived in their house for 30 years and have paid off their mortgage should go out and get a new mortgage and invest the money in the stock market. In some cases that may be appropriate but in most it is not. However, I don't think that the person who is still paying for their home should be in any big hurry to pay the debt down.

Credit card debt is bad debt. One of our clients is a cocktail waitress at a casino. She earns $45,000 a year, half in salary, half in tips. She had $19,000 in credit card debt owed to 12 different credit card companies charging interest of 18 to 21 percent. That's a budget breaker right there. She always paid on time and had good credit—just too much of it. I called the credit card company she owed the most and said, "I've got in my hand a low-rate introductory offer from a rival credit card company good for six months. I am advising my client to move her balance over—unless there is anything you can do to help." They immediately reduced her interest rate from 21 percent down to 12 percent just because we asked. Consider the impact of saving 9 percent on $3,000! Next, I asked the woman if at the end of the month after paying her bills she could come up with $50 or $100. Previously, each month she would use leftover funds to go to a baseball game or dinner out and the money disappeared. I said, "Here is what I want you to do. We have this list of credit card balances. Each month I want you to send an extra $100 dollars to the account with the smallest balance. Make your regular payment, plus the extra $100. After four months, one card will be paid off. After that one is gone, send the next company your regular payment, plus the amount you were paying on the one that is now paid off, plus the extra $100. Keep taking out the small balances first."

The reason she should do that is two-fold.

First, of course, is that it reduces costly interest payments. But second, it provides the client with a real sense of accomplishment. I wanted her to have that. Over a period of two years she could probably get all that debt knocked down. Now, every time I see her she excitedly tells me which cards have been paid off. She took her tax refund and plowed half into paying off credit card debt.

The bad debt has got to go before you start saving. Basically by paying off those credit cards at 18 to 21 percent she's earning an 18 to 21 percent rate of return on that money. That is a handsome return!

As we have seen, debt in itself is not wholly evil—as long as it does not balloon to excessive proportions. I can understand why people finance cars and I don't really have a problem with that. A banker friend, however, recently described a client who earns $3,000 a month who bought a new Chevy Suburban and faces cars payments of $700 a month. That is way too much debt for that gentleman to shoulder.

I don't think clothes should ever be paid for on credit unless you are sufficiently disciplined to pay off the credit card balance every month and incur no finance charges.

Too often, people buy things because they want them, not because they need them. If you look around your house, how much stuff

> **THE BAD DEBT HAS GOT TO GO BEFORE YOU START SAVING. BASICALLY BY PAYING OFF THOSE CREDIT CARDS AT 18 TO 21 PERCENT SHE'S EARNING AN 18 TO 21 PERCENT RATE OF RETURN ON THAT MONEY. THAT IS A HANDSOME RETURN!**

do you have that you wanted but could have lived without?

Curbing your consumer appetites, paying as-you-go for what you buy and avoiding mountainous credit card debt all go hand-in-hand with executing an effective approach to building up one's savings to achieve one's investment strategy.

One of the most readily available tools for saving is the ubiquitous "401(k)" retirement plan offered at most places of employment. For most of us, it will provide a needed supplement to the Social Security payments we receive upon retirement.

MANAGING AND MAXIMIZING YOUR 401(K)

A great percentage of Americans are covered by 401(k), 403(b) or some sort of retirement plan at work. They are one of the best foundations for an investment plan. The reason is simple. The 401(k)s are funded with money that comes out of your paycheck before you can spend it. Unfortunately, for most, that is the only way we will save money. If our salaries flow into a checking account, we will spend it. All of it.

Everyone should have a 401(k). With a 401(k) retirement account, you can grow the money that you are saving each month AND you grow the money that you would otherwise pay in taxes.

If you take $3,000 of earnings in a year and put it into your 401(k) account, that sum immediately starts growing and compounding for you. If you receive the same $3,000 as pay, you are going to give up roughly $1,000—or one-third—in taxes. If you invest the remaining $2,000, it has to grow 50 percent to equal the sum you could have parked—pre-tax—in your 401(k) account.

On top of that, most employers will match a portion of the funds you place into a 401(k). A company may decide to match 50 percent of your investment up to, say, 5 percent of your income. So if you earn, say, $1,000 a week and earmark $50 of it for a 401(k), that $50 will not be subject to federal income tax—and it will trigger an additional 401(k) contribution by your employer of $25—$25 you will not get from your employer if you are NOT in the 401(k)!

401(k)s, clearly, are great for building up one's savings. However, people ALSO do need to save outside their 401(k). They need to be able to have access to some money that is not encumbered by the tax laws—that is to say, money that does not generate a tax bill if it is tapped prior to reaching age 59 ½. If you take funds out of a retirement account before you turn that age, you have to pay the penalty. So what happens if your furnace breaks at your home,

The Bold Truth About Mutual Funds

or if you are confronted with an irresistible business opportunity?

One important note about 401(k)s. Most of us are increasingly mobile in our employment history. When we move from employer to employer, we often can elect to keep our 401(k) in place with our past employer, move it into a new 401(k) with our new employer or simply cash out our investment and receive a check for the sum we have managed to save. Either of the first two options makes good sense. They enable you to proceed with bulking up your savings and sticking to your investment plan. However, way too many of us elect to take a lump-sum payment for the nest egg we have painstakingly built up over the years. This has several negative effects. It triggers a penalty charge and taxes on the proceeds we receive. Perhaps more importantly, it is a retreat in our effort to stay on plan to achieve our financial ambitions.

There is another aspect of being proactive with your 401(k). We must consider the tendency of most of us to forget about tending our 401(k)s. Each of our employers limit the number of investment vehicles open to us in our 401(k)s for an obvious reason: the simplification of our choices was the main way our employer could limit the cost of offering employees a 401(k) option. As we possibly amass several 401(k)s from several employers, we will have a series of investments

HOW TO SHOP FOR A FUND

When I select funds to recommend to our clients at The Mutual Fund Store or to listeners of "The Mutual Fund Show," I do a tremendous amount of due diligence on the fund. I personally talk with the manager, go through the holdings within the fund, read the prospectus, analyze various attribution measures (such as the Sharpe ratio and beta), and look at many other factors. Much of fund selection can be scientific, but there is also a high degree of art.

Most individual investors who select their own funds do not have the time or resources to be as thorough as I am required to be. There are, however, some very basic things you can do to improve your selection methods.

Determine your asset allocation

The first step in determining which funds to own is to decide what sort of fund you are looking for. As I have discussed earlier in this book, it is essential that your investments be split between stocks and bonds, large-cap and small-cap, domestic and international. The asset allocation tells you what kind of funds to own (and in what proportions); the next step is to specifically determine which ones.

Screen for consistency

You can use the free "Quickrank" mutual fund screener at www.Morningstar.com. It is found under the "Tools" tab at the top of the site.

First set the "Fund Category" to the broad asset class that you are seeking, such as Domestic Stocks or Bond Funds. Next, set the "Select Ranking Field" tab to "Total return %: 5-year Annualized". Then click "View Results."

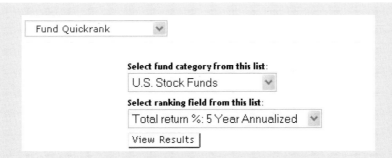

Next, set the "Select Fund Category from this List" tab to the more specific asset class you are looking for; i.e. "Large Cap Growth." This will give you a list of the funds with the highest average returns over the past 5 years.

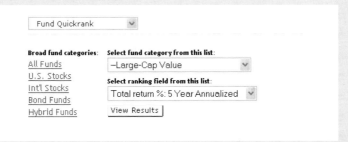

You can not accept the average return as the sole criteria, however. Sometimes a fund will have one year with extraordinarily high returns, which will make the average returns look good, but was really just a function of the manager getting lucky for that one year.

The way to check the consistency is to click on the name of the fund, which will take you to a profile of the fund. Then click on the "Total Returns" tab from the left-hand menu.

You need to look at the calendar-year returns for the fund. Compare the performance each year to that of the appropriate index. Morningstar shows you performance for the past eight years. How many times did the fund beat its benchmark? If the average returns are good but the fund only beat the index half the time, the performance is too "hit or miss" for my taste. If, on the other hand, the fund has beaten the index at least six of the last eight years, it is a candidate for purchase.

Please note that Morningstar shows the performance versus the index or benchmark as a "+/-." In other words, a fund that shows 5.5 versus the index did 5.5% better that year than the index; a negative number means the fund did worse than its benchmark.

Performance History								02-28-05
	1998	1999	2000	2001	2002	2003	2004	02-05
Total return %	---	38.6	8.6	2.8	-16.2	35.2	15.1	1.9
+/- Category	---	18.2	12.9	14.6	5.5	8.0	5.1	2.2
+/- Index	---	17.6	17.7	14.7	5.9	6.6	4.2	2.3
% Rank in Category	---	6	11	3	11	6	6	7

You also should check to see how the fund performed in good years like 1998, 1999, and 2003, and how it did in poor years like 2001 and 2002. There are many funds that did well in one environment or the other, but not in both. There are funds that have been consistent; that is they did better in the good years and they lost less in the bad years. These are the sort of funds we want to own.

Check the manager

After you have found a fund that looks good, you need to make sure that the same manager who was responsible for the past performance is still making the decisions today.

Management

Manager Name	Robert Gardiner
Manager Start Date	06-19-95

Biography

Gardiner is a vice president and director of the Wasatch Advisors, Inc. He joined Wasatch Advisors as an equity analyst in 1987. He is a Chartered Financial Analyst.

You can do that by clicking on the "Management" tab and looking at the manager's tenure. Remember, any performance figures for periods prior to the current manager taking over the fund are irrelevant, because someone else was picking investments for the fund.

Make sure it's a no-load fund

Click on the "Fees & Expenses" tab to see if there are any front or back-end loads. If there are, pick another fund! Incidentally, a redemption fee (as opposed to a deferred sales charge) is OK by me. This is a fee the fund company will charge people who sell the fund within the first few months after purchase. This fee is designed to keep people who rapidly buy and sell funds out, and will protect long-term shareholders over the longer run.

Fees and Expenses

Maximum Sales Fees %

Initial	None
Deferred	None
Redemption	2.00

that were initially made with few choices open to us. While at Company X, we had Mutual Fund A's stock growth fund, bond fund and international stock fund. Then we moved to Company Y and invested our new 401(k) at Mutual Fund B's small capitalization stock growth fund, money market fund and utility fund. Ten years later, we may have $50,000 of our retirement fund tied up in funds offered by Mutual Fund A and Mutual Fund B—even though we no longer work for the employer that directed us to use those funds—and even though those mutual fund products may be dogs.

As we have already established, you owe it to yourself to be in the best funds possible—whether within your 401(k)s or in your overall investment program.

We simply must get proactive about such 401(k)s. The best way to do so is to review the investments with your investment adviser as part of your effort to develop an investment plan.

That review should also extend to any investments we have tumbled into over the years out of ignorance or because we had the ill-fortune to encounter an investment product salesman who did not have our best interests in mind.

AVOID ANY INVESTMENTS YOU DO NOT UNDERSTAND

Life insurance has a simple purpose. It is designed to replace the income of somebody who is no longer with us. I have a wife and three kids. I want to know that if I die tomorrow my wife and children can still live in the same home that we live in now; they can buy groceries; my kids will go to college; my family will enjoy the same lifestyle that they are living now.

It is a simple mathematical formula to figure how much life insurance you need to be able to recreate the income that you have. The best way to achieve that is through term life insurance. If I die they pay my family money. If I don't die they get to keep the premium that I pay them. There's no investment aspect to it; there's no saving for retirement through it. My family's income stream is protected. There's money to pay for the estate taxes on my business. That's it.

However, there are a lot of people out there who will sell life insurance plans as investment vehicles such as variable life insurance. They are almost without exception a bad deal. The way the insurance salesman will sell it to you is he will say, "You can put money into this thing and if you die we will give your family the money. If you don't die, though, this money will go into mutual funds and it will be invested and then it will

> IT IS A SIMPLE MATHEMATICAL FORMULA TO FIGURE HOW MUCH LIFE INSURANCE YOU NEED TO BE ABLE TO RECREATE THE INCOME THAT YOU HAVE. THE BEST WAY TO ACHIEVE THAT IS THROUGH TERM LIFE INSURANCE. IF I DIE THEY PAY MY FAMILY MONEY. IF I DON'T DIE THEY GET TO KEEP THE PREMIUM THAT I PAY THEM.

grow. You will have value there whereas term insurance has no value if it is not used."

When you buy whole life insurance there are several components to the premium. Say that you pay in $100 a month for a life insurance policy. Perhaps $75 of it actually goes to pay for the life insurance, $15 gets invested and the balance covers the insurance company fees. Insurance companies offer 30-year term policies. You buy the insurance today and they guarantee you that rate for the next 30 years. For many people, that's an adequate term. Once your kids are grown and once your house is paid for, the need for replacement income diminishes.

However, while you pay $75 a month—out of your $100 premium—to acquire insurance, a comparable term-policy may cost only $50 a month.

The insurance company, of course, prefers that you pay the higher premium and fees. However, you only get to invest $15 a month. If you buy a term policy for $50 a month, that frees up $50 a month for you to invest—more than three times what you would otherwise set aside!

YOU SHALL SHUN ANNUITIES

Another insurance product to avoid is annuities. The variable annuity is basically a family of mutual funds issued through an insurance company instead of directly by the mutual fund company. Nobody buys an annuity. People are sold annuities. Nobody wakes up in the morning and says, "I think I'll buy an annuity today." Instead some guy comes along and says, "What you need is an annuity!"

Here is how a variable annuity is sold. The insurance agent will tell you that the value of an annuity grows tax-deferred. If you put $100,000 into it today and over the next 10 years it grows to $200,000, there are no taxes on that $100,000 of growth along the way.

This may appeal to someone earning a large income who is not eligible to benefit from a Roth IRA or a tax-deductible IRA.

Many annuities offer a lot of gimmicks to the investor. An insurer could guarantee a return of 3 percent on a mutual fund within an annuity— even in periods when the stock market is down. The devil is in the details. These annuities are sold through a prospectus that is typically 40 or 50 pages thick. I am one of the few people in America who will read a prospectus. After carefully reviewing the literature accompanying annuities, you have to wonder why anyone would buy them.

Here's why: The capital gains tax is now 15 percent for long-term capital gains. That is the highest capital gains rate. Assume that you invest

> NOBODY WAKES UP IN THE MORNING AND SAYS, "I THINK I'LL BUY AN ANNUITY TODAY." INSTEAD SOME GUY COMES ALONG AND SAYS, "WHAT YOU NEED IS AN ANNUITY!"

$100,000 in a mutual fund and that money increases in value over the next several years to $200,000 and then you take the money out. The $100,000 profit is taxed at 15 percent and you are left with a net $185,000.

In an annuity, the growth is tax-deferred. But when you take the money out it is taxed as ordinary income, which can be as high as 35 percent! Consider the same scenario of $100,000 growing to $200,000—except WITHIN an annuity. The $100,000 gain is taxed at 35 percent and you are left with $165,000 after taxes. You've essentially substituted what is likely the lowest tax rate that somebody could pay and you've converted it—through an annuity—into an investment taxed at a very high tax rate.

Clearly, one would sign on for such a proposition only if one fails to understand the specific characteristics of the investment. That is why you should NEVER commit your money to an investment proposition that you do not fully understand. You must take care to be sure that you have an investment adviser who is on YOUR SIDE, willing and capable of fully explaining the various investments open to you and NOT out to steer your money into an investment vehicle that is not in your best interest.

THE END GAME

I work with a lot of people who are retired.
They have been told to save their whole life.

They reach retirement age and I say to them,
"Okay, now what we are going to do is we are
going to start spending your money." Many of
them just can't deal with that. They may point
out, "My account is producing $5,000 a month in
income and if I spend $5,000 a month then it
won't be growing anymore." Well, yes, that's the
idea. But the notion is simply foreign to them.
You may as well tell them to fly to the moon.
Saving has become a habit. Saving has served
them well. Many retirees cannot comfortably
make the psychological transition into spending
their hard-earned savings and investment income.

I will say to them that they can earn 10 percent a year by holding a combination of stocks
and bonds. For some clients that are a little more
risk adverse, maybe we can earn 8 percent. For
a typical 60-year-old who has had stock market
experience and believes he is going to live for an
additional 20 to 30 years, a 10 percent return is a
reasonable investment objective.

Let's consider a hypothetical case. Assume
that we can earn client John Jones 10 percent and
that inflation is going to average 3 percent a year.
Mr. Jones has accumulated $500,000 over his
life time. We can earn him $50,000 a year. Inflation

is going to be at, say, 3 percent. We will tell Mr. Jones that he can spend up to $35,000 a year.

The principal will grow by a sufficient amount over time to increase the sum of money he spends by approximately the rate of inflation. If it costs a dollar to buy a loaf of bread today, 10 years from now we know that it is going to cost more than a dollar. If you can live on $3,000 a month in addition to your Social Security and whatever pension you have, 10 years from now you are going to need more than $3,000 to have the same things—and we take steps to make sure that money will be there.

What do you do if it appears you will not have a sufficient sum to meet your retirement needs? You have two choices. You can accept more volatility over time in exchange for higher returns. Every percentage of higher return that you get is a dollar less that you have to put into the account. Or, you can change your retirement goals.

That could be easier than you may think. First of all, keep in mind that you likely won't be spending as much on taxes and "necessities" when you retire. When you were employed, let's say you were accustomed to living off your specific level of income—typically, your salary. When you have a job, you have to pay Social Security and Medicare tax, which is 7 ½ percent. When you are retired you have to pay income taxes, but you don't have to pay Social Security and Medicare taxes. When you have a job you need to buy work clothes. You may have to put on a suit to go to work. When you are retired you don't have to have those clothes. When you are retired, you will probably put less miles on your car because you are not going to be commuting each day.

If you still see that you'll be coming up short, you could change your lifestyle now so that you save that extra money. One less Saturday night out can save you $50 to $100 dollars a month.

In addition, you may have to change your timelines. You and your adviser may determine that if you work until you are 66 or 67 years old instead of retiring at age 62, you will achieve your goal.

As retirement comes closer, there may be opportunities to tweak your assumptions. If we have a really good year in the stock market, that may get you a little closer to your goal than you expected. For instance, in 1999 when some investments were up 50 percent, we advised some clients close to retirement to take a couple of years' worth of income and place it in a stable money market fund. Then if the market went down, they wouldn't have to worry.

There may be occasions when it makes sense to splurge. After 1999 and 2000 we told some clients planning to buy a car in 2002 to go ahead and advance their plans and buy the car a few years earlier. We told others to take a big trip that they weren't going to take until next year. But we would never say to go out and spend frivolously.

Ultimately, of course, our clients' money is their money. I never tell the client how much to regularly withdraw from their account. That said, however, there are certain common sense considerations for retirees. It makes little sense for them to live their lives in such a manner that they die with a zero net worth. It also is pointless for investors to fully preserve their life savings to transmit to heirs as an inheritance.

Of course, everyone's great fear is that they may run out of money. Again, if you are comfortable assuming some risk associated with investments that will then generate a 10 percent rate of return and you spend 7 percent and reinvest 3 percent, you are going to be fine forever.

Whether you die and leave your children $250,000, $500,000 or $1 million, they should be appreciative. Regardless of what the amount is, it is a bonus for them. On the other hand, if you can do some things in your life before you die that bring you a little more pleasure, I say do it. In all likelihood, your children will be gratified to know your last years were lived—and enjoyed— in grace and comfort.

> **THERE ARE CERTAIN COMMONSENSE CONSIDERATIONS FOR RETIREES. IT MAKES LITTLE SENSE FOR THEM TO LIVE THEIR LIVES IN SUCH A MANNER THAT THEY DIE WITH A ZERO NET WORTH. IT ALSO IS POINTLESS FOR INVESTORS TO FULLY PRESERVE THEIR LIFE SAVINGS TO TRANSMIT TO HEIRS AS AN INHERITANCE.**

Understanding the Mutual Fund Scandals—and Profiting from Change

"HI BARB, THIS IS ADAM BOLD. WHAT'S ON YOUR MIND TODAY?"

"You sounded pretty confident about the future of all of these funds, so I wouldn't have to be watching it very closely or...?."

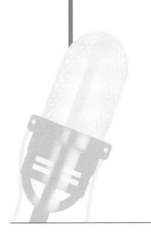

U NDERSTANDING THE MUTUAL FUND SCANDALS—AND PROFITING FROM CHANGE

The stock market meltdown of recent years
was steep and profound. Compared to the
market tumble of 1987, what happened in 2000-
2002 was painful for a huge number of Americans.
I liken the experience to a woman wanting hair
removed from her legs. There are a couple of
ways she could do that. She could have the legs
waxed, in which case the hair is ripped off all at
once. That's the crash of 1987, when we had a
50 percent loss in a two-day period. Or she could
have the hair removed with tweezers, one hair
at a time. That was the bear market of 2000-2002.
Now, neither one is a particularly pleasant
experience. But the worst part about 2000-2002
was not that the market went down, but how
long it lasted.

Everybody learned that asset allocation does
matter. If you have a little bit of this and a little
bit of that, it softens the blow if the market tum-
bles. Some have learned that lesson the hard way
in recent years. Prior to the market collapse, I

had clients with a portfolio of seven to 10 mutual funds and they would say, "I want to sell these bond funds because they're only making 5 or 6 percent. Take all the money and put it into technology funds making 140 percent." I would say, "No, that's not proper asset allocation." They answered, "But that's what I want to do." People got greedy. Their perception of appropriate returns got out of kilter. People were getting mortgages on their houses and investing the proceeds in high-risk, high-volatility stocks.

People—painfully—learned a lot about themselves. Some believed they were long-term investors—only to discover they didn't have the stomach for downturns. When the market went down for 12 months in a row, they said to themselves, "I have got to get out." Others after 24 months of declining stock prices said, "That's it. I have no faith in the stock market. It's never going to come back. I'm gone."

Others continued to hold their stocks 36 months, and then the market finally bounced back. A market bottom is made when the last guy says, "I can't take this anymore. I've got to get out." Once that investor sells, buyers rule the market and stock values start moving up again.

Summing up, what made 2000, 2001, and 2002 different from anything experienced by investors over the last two generations was not the breadth of the declines but rather the long

> EVERYBODY LEARNED THAT ASSET ALLOCATION DOES MATTER. IF YOU HAVE A LITTLE BIT OF THIS AND A LITTLE BIT OF THAT, IT SOFTENS THE BLOW IF THE MARKET TUMBLES. SOME HAVE LEARNED THAT LESSON THE HARD WAY IN RECENT YEARS.

duration of the plunge. It was a rollercoaster that went over the hill, but this one kept plunging ever deeper.

SCAMS A'PLENTY

Compounding the disorientation of investors has been the airing of major problems in the mutual fund sector, where many Americans have parked their investments. It is now clear that pervasive mutual fund scams were going on for quite some time—even prior to the bear market or the bull market of the 1990s. The scandals were a result of people who put the profitability of the companies they worked for or their own financial well-being ahead of the people who were investing in their funds.

THERE COMES A TIME IN A BROKER'S LIFE OR IN THE LIVES OF MUTUAL FUND COMPANY EXECUTIVES WHEN THEY STAND AT A CROSSROADS. THEY CAN DO WHAT IS RIGHT FOR THEIR INVESTORS, OR THEY CAN DO WHAT IS MOST FINANCIALLY BENEFICIAL FOR THEMSELVES OR THEIR COMPANY.

There comes a time in a broker's life or in the lives of mutual fund company executives when they stand at a crossroads. They can do what is right for their investors, or they can do what is most financially beneficial for themselves or their company. A broker, considering his options, may say to himself, "This is an IRA account and I can sell the client a mutual fund that has a 5 percent load or I can sell him an annuity that has a 7 percent load. If it's a $100,000 account, I'm going to make $7,000 instead of making $5,000 by pushing the annuity. I'll take the $7,000." We have been reminded of late that many trusted advisers are willing to make that calculation.

High-ranking executives are certainly not immune to compromising their ethics. More than a few mutual fund executives thought to themselves, "We have a prospectus which is a legal document that tells the shareholders in these funds what they can expect in service and the rules of investing with us. We can either follow those rules or we can make a special deal with certain other special investors, ignore our rules and earn my firm a few extra million dollars a year. I'll do that."

In turn, several kinds of scams emerged in the recent mutual fund scandals. One involved late trading. When you buy a mutual fund, regardless of what time you place your order—whether it's at 7 a.m. or 2 p.m., the time does not matter—the price that you will pay for shares you are buying or the sum you will receive for shares you are selling is based on the closing price of each of the underlying shares. You must place your order by 4 p.m. Eastern time. However, a few preferred clients with hefty accounts were allowed to place orders to buy mutual funds as late as 6 p.m. Some of these individuals actually had written arrangements with some of the mutual funds spelling out their privileges.

Frequently corporations will wait until after the close of trading on the stock market to make

an announcement about an important develop-
ment likely to affect the price of their stock. It
could be an earnings announcement, or word
that they are being acquired by another company. Disclosing these matters after market close
can take some of the volatility out of trading
company stock, because it does not allow
investors to speculate wildly about what may
be happening.

Let's say you had a mutual fund that owned
shares of Intel, and after the close Intel reported
that its earnings for the quarter stood at $1 a
share and stock analysts had for weeks forecast
earnings of 80 cents a share. In all likelihood,
Intel shares would trade higher the next day,
because the earnings were dramatically higher
than what people had expected. If you are in a
position to buy the stock based on today's price
knowing that information, then you are certain
to profit the next day when trading opens.

Assume that Intel was selling for $20 a share,
and based on that information it climbed to $25
a share the next day. That $5-per-share profit
should have been split between the people who
owned that mutual fund prior to 4 p.m. the
previous day. Instead, that $5 profit is now split
between the people who owned the fund prior to
4 p.m. the previous day and the privileged few
people who were able to buy the shares after
the close of business. They were dealing with

perhaps a $100 million investment. If they can make one-half of a percent in one day on that amount of money, it's a great deal.

POLICY, NOT ABERRATION

It is one thing if a lone guy who worked for a mutual fund allowed this to happen. It's a scandal when a mutual fund's management develops written policies condoning the practice of late trading. Indeed, that did occur.

Why would a mutual fund company allow this to happen? Because it paid off. The fund would make a deal with large investors in which the investors are allowed to occasionally engage in late trading. In exchange, the investor would make large investments—say $500 million—in one of the mutual fund company's bond funds. These funds were considered "sticky" in that the money would remain parked in the account for long periods of time. The mutual fund company would earn the day-to-day investment management fees on the $500 million in exchange for letting the investors make $100 million worth of late trades from time to time in their stock funds.

Another scandalous practice that developed at some of the mutual fund companies, time zone arbitrage, took advantage of the opportunity to trade stocks globally. It worked this way: Assume the markets closed lower in Europe and the U.S.

ANOTHER SCANDALOUS PRACTICE THAT DEVELOPED AT SOME OF THE MUTUAL FUND COMPANIES, TIME ZONE ARBITRAGE, TOOK ADVANTAGE OF THE OPPORTUNITY TO TRADE STOCKS GLOBALLY.

CASE STUDY No. 7

A couple had been doing business for several years with a stockbroker who attended their church. They had enjoyed a good relationship with the broker and felt comfortable with him on a personal level. But after several years of under-performance they were questioning whether they should make a change and hire someone else to manage their investments.

This is a situation almost every investor will deal with at some point because there is always the temptation to wonder: "Could I be doing better?" At the same time it is important to maintain a good relationship with whoever is handling your investments because of the level of trust involved. There are two reasons to switch brokers and it is up to the individual investor to determine at what point they will make a change. The first reason is if the performance of your investments isn't matching your expectations and the second is if you have a poor relationship with your adviser.

In this particular case the couple decided to make a switch despite their personal feelings about him. They sat down and explained their reasons, which was very difficult to do. Having a solid relationship with your adviser is important but in this particular case they decided they were sacrificing too much in the way of performance to continue.

CONCLUSION

No matter who is handling your investments it is important to remember it is your money and you are paying for a service. If you feel you're not getting the results you deserve you need to consider making changes. The relationship you have worked to develop with your adviser can make it difficult to switch fund managers, but it is important to remember you are dealing with your money and your financial future. The most important thing to being a smart investor is making intelligent decisions; don't let emotions prevent you from making the best choice.

markets then opened lower in the morning. Then some event sparked a big rally. One can assume with a high degree of probability that when the markets then opened in Europe the next day, they would be higher following the trend of the U.S. markets. A handful of select mutual fund clients were allowed to frequently buy an international fund and then capture profit that they knew was coming in the international markets overseas. That's not illegal; however, most mutual fund companies in their prospectus set out a policy that prohibits frequent trading of their mutual funds. Frequent trading hurts the long-term shareholders. In reality, if large sums flow into a mutual fund and are only there for one day, the mutual fund manager doesn't have time to place them into stock investments. That money is just getting money-market returns. Meanwhile, the profits that the existing shareholders are entitled to are spread among the existing shareholders and the short-term investors. That is why many mutual funds allow investors to only buy and sell fund shares several times a year.

Unfortunately, several mutual fund companies violated their own written rules; mutual fund executives signed written agreements with special investors allowing them to make hundreds of trades a year in a fund. In exchange, the special investors may have agreed to park large sums in one of the fund company's bond funds.

In a couple of instances, principals in the mutual fund were forced to resign. At Strong Funds, for example, founder and chairman Dick Strong was engaging in frequent trading inside his own personal account and was forced to sell his mutual fund company. At the MFS Family Funds (Massachusetts Financial Services), the nation's first mutual fund company, the president and CEO were actually banned from the investment industry for a year. At PBHG Funds (Pilgrim and Baxter), two of the principals of the fund were forced to resign from the fund company.

Those have really been the exceptions. The more common outcome has been that the mutual fund firms paid some sort of restitution to the shareholders who were harmed; they paid a fine, agreed to clean up their act, and have since moved on. The vast majority of the executives who permitted questionable and unethical activities are still in their positions. Thus, I cannot recommend leaving money in those fund companies or putting new money with those fund companies.

DANGERS STILL AHEAD

My father told me when I was a kid, "You're either a gentleman or you're not. You can't go back and forth." I still can be friends with somebody who is not a gentleman, but I'm certainly not going to go into business with them. I know people in this world who, when given a choice between doing things the right way and doing things the sneaky way, will do it the sneaky way even if the right way is easier. That's just their nature.

When it comes to mutual fund companies, I recognize that after all we've been through with the regulators and publicity about unethical behavior, the types of problems we've seen in recent years are not likely to continue at the offending companies. However, what will happen the next time that one of these mutual fund companies is presented with an opportunity to do something that maybe isn't illegal, isn't in their customers' best interest but is financially advantageous to the mutual fund company and its executives? I have no confidence that people who have made sneaky decisions one time are going to make a right decision the next time they stand at an ethical crossroads.

There are 12 to 15 mutual fund companies today that I refuse to deal with. There are enough other companies out there that have always acted ethically and whose first concern is for the well-being of their shareholders.

Most investors have already pushed the problems of the mutual fund industry from their minds. But they shouldn't. There are other issues that are horrendously wrong in the mutual fund industry that have come to light but have not received deserved attention.

For example, many brokerage houses maintain a select list of funds and they tell customers, "This is our preferred list of mutual funds." If I was a customer and was presented such a list, I would assume it meant that the firm had done some sort of research and had determined that these were the best funds out there. As it turns out, in some cases, a fund made it onto the list because the mutual fund company paid the brokerage firm a hefty $500,000 to $1 million fee plus a portion of the ongoing management fees of the fund. This has been happening at a number of firms.

Brokers that work for the brokerage firm are free to sell any mutual fund with which their company has a selling agreement—and not just the ones that are on the preferred list. The reality is

THERE ARE **12 TO 15** MUTUAL FUND COMPANIES TODAY THAT **I** REFUSE TO DEAL WITH. THERE ARE ENOUGH OTHER COMPANIES OUT THERE THAT HAVE ALWAYS ACTED ETHICALLY AND WHOSE FIRST CONCERN IS FOR THE WELL-BEING OF THEIR SHAREHOLDERS.

that the brokers are encouraged by management to sell the preferred list, and in most cases the majority of the firm's mutual fund sales come from the list.

I don't agree with that practice, but believe it is not illegal—as long as customers are told by their brokers, "The way that this fund made it to the preferred list is that the fund company paid a bunch of money to my company." But obviously, that disclosure is never made to investors. I suspect that almost every large brokerage house has an agreement with certain mutual fund companies.

Some brokerages are captive companies. Brokers are only allowed to sell the brokerage's own mutual funds. I can assure you that no one fund company has a monopoly on all the best funds.

Thus, you must ask yourself why you are holding a number of funds all under one mutual fund company umbrella. You must always be mindful of the performance of each and every fund that you own.

What amazes me about this is that there are billions of dollars that are sitting in horrendous funds. Some of them are in no-load funds and some are load funds. Consider a no-load fund like the Vanguard U.S. Growth Fund, VUSGX, that holds more than $1 billion. It has continually been in the bottom 10 or 15 percent of all funds

Over time various funds open and close, but on occasion people will notice a fund closes to new investors but remains active for those who already have purchased it. New investors want to know what causes funds to close like this, and people who already own part of this fund might be worried that this is the sign of a problem. While these concerns are understandable, it's usually a good sign when a fund closes to new investors.

Fund managers close a fund because they are bringing in so many assets that they're afraid they won't be able to deliver the type of results they are currently giving their clients. Statistically, small funds perform better than large funds. Certain SEC regulations governing mutual funds force larger funds to be spread wider and be more diversified than small funds. A manager may have identified a number of companies he or she believes are wise investments, but as the fund grows the manager is forced to look at other companies, and as a result invest in areas they do not feel as strongly about.

Also, it is possible for a fund to reach a point where it is unwieldy and difficult to control. When clients choose to purchase a fund, the manager must then find a way to invest the cash. They sometimes might not see any options in the market that fit the profile of the particular fund. A good manager will be able to recognize a fund approaching a point where the performance may have to be sacrificed in order to allow more investors.

CONCLUSION

When a manager chooses to close a fund to new investors, it normally indicates two good things. First, it shows that the manager knows how to structure a strong fund and is capable of managing it properly. Second, it is an indication of good ethical behavior. The manager is risking turning away some new clients in order to better serve the investors that have already trusted him or her with their money.

out there. Clearly, the marketplace is not efficient because if it were, people would pull their money out of such funds and their managers would be out of business.

RETIREMENT PLANNING IS YOUR JOB

As an investor, it is your responsibility to either pay greater attention to your investments or hire people capable of doing it for you. During the bull market of 1996 through 1999, people thought it was easy. They could just buy anything. A bad fund went up 15 percent. The

AS AN INVESTOR, IT IS YOUR RESPONSIBILITY TO EITHER PAY GREATER ATTENTION TO YOUR INVESTMENTS OR HIRE PEOPLE CAPABLE OF DOING IT FOR YOU.

bear market and subsequent recovery showed that picking winners over the long term is hard.

Incredibly, there are people still holding funds they bought in the late 1990s containing the securities of Internet companies that have gone bust, hoping that those funds come back. Some investors say, "I put $10,000 into this fund. Now it's worth $5,000. I know it's an Internet fund and it's bad but I'm going to hold it until it goes back to $10,000 and then I'll do something different." One should not always look backward. It doesn't matter what you bought in the past. That cannot be undone. What counts is a thorough, honest assessment of what you have today. Do you own the best investments possible that will perform well in the future?

You have no option but to think in these terms if you want a healthy income when you retire. The Social Security retirement system will not make it the way that it's run right now. Period. I can say that with absolute certainty because of demographics. Demographics also show that the stock market will do well for the next 15-20 years. The Baby Boomers born between 1946 and 1964 are the largest single population group in the United States today, amounting to approximately 30 percent of the total population. As Social Security currently works, you've got three working people making Social Security payments supporting every person receiving benefits. The Baby Boomers are working and supporting their retired parents. When the Baby Boomers start to retire and draw Social Security, the numbers don't work anymore because there will not be three workers behind each retiree.

The federal government can raise the retirement age so that there is more time for this money to accumulate before the Baby Boomers start pulling money out. With Americans living longer, that is a reasonable approach.

Furthermore, people should have the opportunity to invest a portion of their Social Security contributions in the stock market. This concept has been proposed by political leaders in recent years and has resurfaced in the Bush administration. If we move to such a system, the government will probably give workers the opportunity to place their money in stock index funds tracking the performance of a large number of companies. That would create an opportunity to save the Social Security system, because the rates of return that workers would receive would help boost their retirement payments. Currently, the funds that the government collects for Social Security are placed into the U.S. Treasury and spent on federal programs. If the money is placed into the stock market, that would have the added benefit of creating pressure on the government to curb spending

> **PEOPLE SHOULD HAVE THE OPPORTUNITY TO INVEST A PORTION OF THEIR SOCIAL SECURITY CONTRIBUTIONS IN THE STOCK MARKET.**

Now let's return to the matter of demographics. When the Baby Boomers go from being net savers to net spenders, who is going to buy their stocks? Another troubling question: who will buy their large homes? Baby Boomers throughout their lives have continually upgraded their housing. Currently, the people at the front end of the Baby Boom generation are selling their bigger houses to the people at the back end. Well, when the number of buyers goes down, who is going to buy my house? There's not going to be enough people to buy houses in the way that they have thus far.

The good news is, at the same time that the ranks of Baby Boomers are peaking, there are other places in the world where a new Baby Boom generation is coming of age. That is happening in India, China and across Latin America. Hopefully there will be an army of investors outside of the United States interested in acquiring our investments. And possibly a new wave of upwardly mobile immigrants to America will increase demand for residential real estate.

No one knows. One thing is certain. In coming decades you as a diligent, smart investor will have to be very strategic and alert to macroeconomic and demographic shifts. Everything that we've learned over the last 30 years of investing will be replaced by an entirely new set of insights.

The Bold Truth About Mutual Funds

Fund Manager Interviews

Rick Lane
FMI FOCUS

David Williams
EXCELSIOR VALUE
AND RESTRUCTURING

Brian Barish
CAMBIAR
OPPORTUNITY

Anton Schutz
BURNHAM
FINANCIAL SERVICES

ADAM BOLD FEATURES PROMINENT MANAGERS OF MUTUAL FUNDS ON HIS WEEKLY RADIO SHOW. HERE ARE A FEW OF ADAM'S MOST INTERESTING INTERVIEWS.

ICK LANE

FMI Focus

ADAM   My guest on the show this week is Rick Lane. Rick is the manager of the FMI Focus Fund, and Rick, I want to thank you again for being with us once more on *The Mutual Fund Show.*

RICK   *Thanks for having me Adam.*

ADAM   Rick, as a refresher, tell us about the basic investment philosophy for the FMI Focus Fund.

RICK   *Well, as you recall, Adam, we focus on small and mid-sized companies. We look for companies that tend to be out of the limelight. Our investment strategy is two pronged. We want to buy companies that sell at least the 25% discount to private market value, which is basically the price another company in that same industry would likely pay if they were to buy that company lock, stock, and*

The Bold Truth About Mutual Funds

barrel. We also like to see a company be in a
strategic position within that industry, so obviously
it would be of some interest to other players within
the industry. Those are the two major tenants on
the evaluation side.

Now, on the other side of the equation, of course,
we want to see earnings per share of growth or
growth in franchise value because at the end of the
day most companies don't get taken over. Certainly
we have a fair amount that do get taken over as a
byproduct of our formula but at the end of the day
you really need growth and earnings per share or
in franchise value. So we look at both sides of the
equation there. I would tell you quickly that a great
example of that, which was a happy thing for our
investors here, was when Allegiant Bank in St.
Louis was bought out by National City recently.
That was a terrific situation for us.

Rick, one of the criteria that you have for   **ADAM**
buying a stock is that the company have a
catalyst. Can you explain the concept of
a catalyst?

Absolutely. A catalyst is a reason for the stock   **RICK**
to go up. One of the problems I have always found
with pure value investing is that it's one thing to
buy a company that looks undervalued and the
assets would be worth much more than would be
stated on the books, but if there's not a catalyst or

a reason to propel that stock forward it's not very interesting. A lot of companies sell below private market value but there may not be any event such as new product flow, earnings growth, things of that nature that would get the stock moving and be of interest to investors, and that can be the classic value trap which is what we try to avoid.

ADAM   Your fund, the FMI Focus Fund, has beaten the overall market every year of its existence except for 2002 when you underperformed by the whopping amount of ⁹⁄₁₀ of 1%. What do you think has been the key to your success?

RICK   *Well, I think that our investment strategy is durable. At the end of the day a lot of strategies come into vogue and then go out of vogue. Sometimes small cap stocks are in vogue. Sometimes big cap stocks are in vogue. Sometimes the value stocks are in vogue. Sometimes growth stocks are in vogue. I think our two pronged investment strategy, which is looking for companies that sell at a discount to private market value but also show earnings growth potential, always works in most environments.*

It gets back to good old stock picking and bottom up analysis but at the end of the day I think our investment strategy is a durable one that works in a lot of different environments, and so far so good. The fund is just over seven years old right now and we've lived through a lot of different investment environments, as your listeners know full well, and I think that our strategy has shown to be quite durable through lots of different scenarios.

ADAM

Do you choose an industry or a sector that you want to invest in and then find stocks in that sector or do you just find great companies and you don't really care what industry they're in?

RICK

Well, it's definitely some of both. If you recall about a year and a half ago, we thought that there were going to be ownership changes in the media and we bought a bunch of companies like Young Broadcasting, Hurst Argyle, Emmis Communications, and that was really twofold. One, we thought that, as you know Adam, advertising is very cyclical and we were betting the economy was going to improve. So we thought advertising as an environment would improve. Secondly, we thought that we would start to get some consolidation with changes in the media laws, which I think are about to happen as we speak here. So that got us looking at media stocks as a group. So that would be more of a top down scenario.

Just as often, though, we'll be looking pure bottom up. For instance, one of our favorite stocks right now, a company called Unova, is a company that makes bar code scanning equipment, and if you're familiar with the concept of RFID, Radio Frequency Identification, it is going to be a huge growth area and Unova is one of the few pure plays in that arena. So that would be another example of just a pure bottom up idea.

ADAM   Rick, small cap stocks had a great year in 2003 and 2004. What's your view today? Are there still bargains out there?

RICK   *That's the great thing about small cap. There are so many small cap companies. You can always find something. I would say, though, that it is clearly getting more challenging. If you identified, we have had 14 or 15 months of pretty strong performance in small cap land and a lot of stocks, I think, are approaching fully valued. So you have to be more selective. Towards that end, because we do do some work in the mid cap arena, I'm actually finding more value in the mid cap area and we've actually been doing more investing in that area. So I think what you point out is valid. Fortunately though, in small cap land there are probably 5 to 10,000 companies to choose from and lots of companies going public and when they start their life they're small cap. So it's always kind of renewing itself, too, but what you say I think is valid. You have to be more selective now.*

ADAM So part of what you're saying is that the easy money has been made in the market, at least with this part of the stock market recovery. Now it's going to become a little more challenging and certainly having a good fund manager who knows what he's doing is going to make even more difference going forward.

RICK *Oh, absolutely, and I think that you have to tone down your expectations a little bit, too. As you know, the FMI Focus Fund was up 48% in 2003. That would be a very unfair expectation every year.*

ADAM I expect you to do double that this year, Rick.

RICK *Ah, thanks Adam. I think this year will be a positive year. It is a presidential election year. The economy is improving but I don't think it will be anything like last year. I think you just simply have to tone down your expectations somewhat, and you're right: stock selection is going to be a lot more important this year. I think that last year you probably could have thrown a dart at the dart board and made a lot of money. It'll be a lot harder this year.*

ADAM Rick, one of the things that we've seen over the last year or so is that a number of small cap funds have actually closed to new investors because there was so much new money coming into the funds that the mangers found it increasingly difficult to find new stocks to buy. Tell me about the status of the FMI Focus Fund in terms of new asset flows, the size of the fund itself and whether you would ever consider closing the fund to new investors.

RICK   *The size of the fund now is about $1.2 billion. It has grown substantially and, of course, part of that is simply the fact that we were up 48% in 2003, but we did take in a fair amount of new money last year and towards year end we had a meeting at the firm and we decided that if those flows were going to continue at such a strong pace, we were pre-pared to close the fund. We have done all the things that we need to do from a formal planning process to accomplish that goal quickly if we need to.*

Fortunately, new cash flow into the fund has slowed down almost to a trickle, and notwithstand-ing the fact that I'm a businessman and I've always liked to see my assets under management grow, I'm actually happy that has happened because there are lots of reasons why you would like to keep your fund open for new investors if you can, but if we do get to the point where we feel that we're being overwhelmed with new cash flow, we are prepared to slow it down. But at this point Adam, I would say that I don't think I'm going to have to do it anytime soon with a caveat that if the new cash flow does start to come in, we will take that action.

Here's an important question that I ask every fund manager that I have on the show and that is, do you personally have money invested in your fund? **ADAM**

Yes, I'm very happy to say that it is by far my largest personal financial asset and I can say that about most of the members of our team here. In fact, we have a rule that I think most firms ought to have that says the people who work for Broadview Advisors can not invest in individual common stocks. All of their exposure to the stock market needs to be through formal products that we manage as a firm. So yes, it is a huge asset for me. **RICK**

You know, it's always interesting to me and the reason I ask that question is because I figure if you have your money in there you're going to be more concerned about it than if you didn't, but they get these analysts on CNBC and they will say, "Well, do you own this stock or does anybody in your family own the stock?" And they very proudly say, "No." Well, it seems to me that you'd feel better if the guy did own the stock. **ADAM**

Yeah, I couldn't agree more. That's the funny thing, but the legal environment has gotten to be so tricky I guess I can understand that attitude, but it is also one of the reasons why we tend to be much more cautious, particularly in bad environments. **RICK**

We have a willingness to raise high cash levels when we have concerns about valuation of the market or we simply can't find stocks that meet our criteria. We don't force it and we're willing to let cash levels build very often to the chagrin of investment advisers because they like their mutual fund managers to run fully invested. But again, because I have a lot of my own personal assets in the money, I tend to treat it very carefully.

ADAM Rick, is there anything else you'd like to tell my listeners?

RICK *Well, to the extent that I know that many of your listeners are shareholders and we thank you for that, we take every shareholder very seriously and if you do have any questions whatsoever please don't hesitate to contact us.*

ADAM My guest on the show has been Rick Lane, manager of the FMI Focus Fund and Rick, I want to thank you not only for being with us here on *The Mutual Fund Show* but also for the great job that you've done for our clients at *The Mutual Fund Store* and for my listeners to *The Mutual Fund Show*.

RICK *Adam, I appreciate your having me on. It's always a pleasure.*

DAVID WILLIAMS
Excelsior Value and Restructuring

My guest this week is David Williams. David is the manager of the Excelsior Value and Restructuring Fund, and David, I want to thank you for being with us today. **ADAM**

You're welcome Adam. **DAVID**

David, first of all tell us about your core investment philosophy. **ADAM**

I like to say that we invest in companies when they're in trouble and we sell them when they're out of trouble, when they fix the problem, and we invest in companies that are restructuring that we think have good long-term values that are cheap, in other words, and we look at the normal PE ratios and the metrics that other people look at and we just take a very long-term view of what we invest in. We have very low turnover. We tend to **DAVID** *have a little higher dividend yield than the market. So I think it's a conservative portfolio, one that weathers pretty well in all kinds of environments.*

ADAM   Because the market has dropped so precipitously, are there a lot of stocks that we used to consider growth companies that have now fallen into the value range?

DAVID   *I think that's less true now than it was six to eight months ago, but sure, I think it's always a moving target and where do you draw the line. Only the consultants seem to worry too much about what's growth and what's value. I just look at companies for the parameters that I look for and if they are cheap I buy them. If they're not I pass and they may be value. They may be growth but I think typically they would be defined as value stocks. One measure that is my average PE in my portfolio is, for next year's earnings, about 12 ½ times and next year's earnings for the S&P sells at about 17 ½ times. So that's about a 30% discount or so and that's typically what I look for.*

ADAM   So do you choose an industry or a sector that you want to invest in and then find stocks in that sector or do you work from the bottom up?

DAVID   *Kind of the latter. Usually I just find a company that is attractive and take a position, but you know what Adam, it's oftentimes when one company in a sector or industry is attractive oftentimes the other* *ones are as well. So in that way, even by a bottoms up process, you can work yourself into an over-weighed position.*

What has made this year's returns so much different from last year?

ADAM

What's going on here, I think it's very simple in my opinion anyway even though it's not palpable perhaps just yet and certainly there's some unemployment, that recovery is here, and I think especially important was the fact that we had this tax policy that encouraged investors to buy dividend yielding stocks and to take some capital gains and it just was very, very pro stock market, the tax laws that we had enacted this year. I think that's huge, but essentially the market seems to follow earnings and earnings last year were flat-ish and uncertain. This year I think there's a much, much better visibility and earnings are really coming back very, very nicely. So it's not surprising that the market is doing better this year. Having said that, the market always surprises. We climb a wall of worry, as they say, and it sure looks like a lot of the good news has been discounted but let's see what happens.

DAVID

Well, I always say that a bear market turns around when you least expect it. I mean certainly we didn't have Tom Brokaw come on the news and say, "Okay, the bear market

ADAM

is over. It's time to buy stocks again."

DAVID   *Right. Right.*

ADAM   And of course it always feels different when it's going on and it's only with hindsight that you realize that it really wasn't that much different than what we've seen in the past.

DAVID   *As they say, a bell doesn't go off at the bottom and a bell doesn't go off at the top and that's certainly the case. Although I agree with you Adam, but I think this time, if I can remember those—I mean I was so depressed about six to eight months ago about what was going on—but I just think it reached such an extreme and the smartest people, the smartest economists and the smartest market analysts that I follow really were saying, "This thing is way overdone. The market was oversold." I never say I told you so but I just had a good feeling that this market was going to do really, really good. It just was much too pessimistic about six to eight months ago.*

ADAM   As you said, corporate earnings have been pretty good for the last couple of quarters. A lot of the gains, though, come from cost cutting rather than top line growth. I mean there's two ways that a company can increase their earnings. One is to sell more and the other is to cut expenses. Do you think that we're going

to see a time in the not-too-distant future
when the actual sales are going to start growing?

DAVID

*Well, I think it's spotty still but I think they
are. Maybe that's wishful thinking but no; I
sense that certainly in certain industries the top
line is growing very nicely. Especially the cyclicals. The problem is the industrials, the manufacturing sector. I think everything else is looking pretty good and the manufacturing sector
has its own—and I think it's going to come
back—but it has its own problems. I think it's
being displaced obviously to one or another,
globally. Personally I think that's a little bit overdone by the media. I think that certain industries within the manufacturing sector, if you will,
are having more trouble with that. Our strong
point has always been computers and software
and technology and things like that. I think
we're probably still hanging in there.*

ADAM

Yeah, but I always say that if you've got an
object, let's say a ball point pen, there's no
reason that that needs to be made in America
where you've got a worker getting $30 an hour
and getting every holiday and their birthday
off and health benefits and everything else. On
the other hand, if I'm in a car wreck and have
to be on a ventilator that's going to keep me

alive, I'd just as soon have an HP or a Johnson & Johnson rather than something made in Malaysia.

DAVID   *Well, I agree with you. I mean I definitely agree with your sentiment. For example, I own the Ford Converts (convertible bonds) and I buy Ford cars just to help out American manufacturing, at least what little I can do to help things along. I believe in buying American if the product is just as good. A lot of people would debate if our products are just as good, but as you say, certain areas…*

ADAM   We're just better at it than others.

DAVID   *…especially technology related, our products are great and we're manufacturing them here.*

ADAM   Yeah, I mean there are certain things that we're just better at making than other people are.

DAVID   *Right. This is basic economics and people don't get it through their thick skull, especially in the media. I think a lot of what you hear in the medial is politically driven and I really do think that the economy, if they just would leave it alone, is going to do great. Yes, there will be some job displacements along the way but that's very, very healthy.*

ADAM   What sort of things are you buying now?

DAVID   *I tell you what, I'm saying with the cyclicals,* *and I know that's a very, very broad category and I think it's becoming much too consensus oriented. That makes me a little bit nervous but I do think to the extent that, again as I said, the market problems, the earnings, I think the earnings will be with the cyclicals. Again, kind of hard for me to generalize but I don't think you've seen a lot of the earnings yet in that category. So as a broad generalization I guess I'm saying with the cyclicals.*

Here's a question that I ask every mutual fund manager that I have on the show and that is, do you personally have money invested in your fund?   **ADAM**

Oh, yeah. I have a lot of my retirement. I think I have over $300,000 of my retirement plan in it.   **DAVID**

So you care whether it goes up or down?   **ADAM**

Oh, sure. Sure. But you know what? In our business you don't have the time to worry about your own account that much, and I really don't. I just put it in there and I don't even think about it.   **DAVID**

So it's kind of like the cobbler's children have no shoes?   **ADAM**

Yeah, exactly, you got it. That's exactly right and so I don't worry about it. They don't let us buy stocks that are in the fund. There are all kinds of restrictions and so forth so I don't even give it   **DAVID** *a second thought.*

ADAM   Is there anything else that you'd like to tell
my listeners?

DAVID   *I guess we're all thinking about the market and
is it a propitious time to add money to equities and
I really do not have the answer Adam, but I think
the market is becoming fairly valued. I think it's
going to be a little bit tougher for the market to go
up. On the other hand, I say the fundamentals I
think are improving and maybe the market is going
to overshoot and I think the earnings next year are
going to be very good. So I just would be a little bit
more even keel in your approach and not put all
your eggs in one basket. I would recommend that
they do that and the bond market has been kind of
weak. Maybe at some point you want to take a, if
you don't have any bonds in your portfolio maybe
you want to do something there, but I just think the
situation obviously is so much different now than it
was six to eight months ago.*

ADAM   Of course, I think what you're saying is the
easy money has been made in the market.

DAVID   *Yeah. I think most people would agree
with that.*

ADAM   But would you also agree that if you put
money into the market now, five years from
now you'll probably be pretty happy you did?

The Bold Truth About Mutual Funds

DAVID

Yes, I believe that very strongly. If there was one thing that everyone had missed last year was that in the long-term the market is still going to do fine.

ADAM

I contend that the worst part about this bear market that we had from 2000 through the beginning of 2003 or end of 2002 was not so much that the market went down because everybody knew that sometimes things went down on the way to going up, but rather it just lasted so long that it tested people's persistence.

DAVID

Yes.

ADAM

That there were a certain number who could take six months of a down market and there was another subset that could take a year and another subset that could take two years and when it got to three years people just said, "I thought I was a long-term investor but I guess I'm not."

DAVID

I have a lot of individual clients and I think where we had trouble last year was where people just got too, and partly my fault I'm the first to admit it, but what we had were too aggressive an equity position and where they just didn't have the wealth to carry them over for the three year bear market that we had. That's where we ran into trouble. I think the people that did best were people that just forgot about the market and went about their business and had the confidence and didn't need the cash flow incidentally, and had the confidence that it was going to come back. Those peoples are sitting pretty right now. The people that got worried and cashed out of the market and put it into bonds, those people again they're getting whip sawed, and that's not what you want to do in our business.

ADAM   And of course the media exacerbated that because 10 years ago you didn't have CNBC reporting on every single tic of the market. They'd get the analyst on and they'd go, "Yeah, the market is down 15 points today. Why?" I mean give me a break.

DAVID   *Yeah. I've been asked a number of times to do shows and talk about what I thought the market was going to do that day and I said, "You know what, that's the least of my worries." I don't know what it's going to do, number one, and even if I thought I did I wouldn't do a very good job. It's a very, very difficult thing to do but they need that filler for their programs. So I pass on those programs. I don't like to talk to them just because I don't think I'm being honest with the listeners.*

ADAM   Well, David, I want to thank you, first of all, for being with me today and I also want to thank you for the great job that you've done for me...

You're welcome.   **DAVID**

...for my clients, for my listeners of the show.   **ADAM**
You've just been a real gem and I have a
tremendous amount of respect for you and
your abilities.

Thank you very much. I appreciate it.   **DAVID**

All right. That was my guest David Williams,   **ADAM**
manager of the Excelsior Value and
Restructuring Fund. I'm your host, Adam
Bold, and we'll be right back.

BRIAN BARISH

Cambiar Opportunity

ADAM   My guest on the show this week is Brian Barish. He is a co-manager of the Cambiar Opportunity Fund, and Brian, I want to thank you for taking time to be with us today.

BRIAN   *Well, thank you very much. I appreciate the opportunity.*

ADAM   Tell us about the basic investment philosophy for the Cambiar Opportunity Fund.

Brian   *Certainly. We are a relative value manager. That is our style and philosophy. What we're looking to do is to mitigate the risk considerations of any of our investments by buying stocks that we think have good value characteristics, such that they are not very expensive for what they do, yet are in good industries with favorable dynamics that over time should show some growth characteristics. It's a "good companies at good prices" philosophy. If our stocks happen to become expensive relative to what we think are reasonable expectations for the company then we sell them.*

Brian, because the market dropped so precipitously in 2000 through 2002, are there a lot of companies out there that we used to consider growth companies that have now sort of fallen into the value range?

ADAM

There definitely are. I would caution any listener to this program that just because a stock is down, it doesn't mean that it's a value. A lot of stocks got to comical, outrageous valuations at the height of the bubble and the magnitude of it is really hard to fully comprehend but there are certainly many that fall into that category. As an illustration, one of the larger positions in our fund today is Microsoft. Well, that company clearly was one of the champions of the technology bull market of the 1990s and is not the high growth machine that it was 10 years ago. But it's still a very wonderful franchise. They're very cash generative and what we try to do is stay as unemotional as possible about assessing all of the investment candidates in our fund.

BRIAN

If you look at Microsoft and you forget what they do and you forget what the company's history is and just look at the pure financial characteristics, we think it's very interesting. Microsoft sells

*for $25. They have about $6 a share in cash and
cash equivalent. So excluding that position $19 a
share is about what you're really paying for the
business and that business is going to generate
about $1.40 to $1.50 per share in free cash flow in
the upcoming 12 months. That's a free cash flow
yield of about 8 percent. That's a very high free
cash flow yield no matter what that company does.
In the case of Microsoft they're growing at about
a 10, maybe 12 percent rate going forward. We
think that's reasonable. That's a very attractive
investment and we're buyers.*

ADAM   When you're looking for stocks, do you choose
an industry or sector that you want to invest in
and then find stocks in that sector or do you
just find companies you like and go that way?

BRIAN   *We are more the latter. We consider ourselves
to be bottoms up. We're looking for companies
that have attractive financial characteristics that
are in businesses that we like but which happen to
be cheap. We don't take a top-down view of the
market and then pick our stocks accordingly. Now,
that much said, we're not oblivious to the top-down
consideration. So as an illustration, in my opinion,
we're poised to see interest rates rise fairly mean-
ingfully in the next couple of years and there are a
number of industries, like homebuilding for example, mortgage lenders and so forth, that*

*are very sensitive to interest rates. A lot of those
companies have seen inflated levels of business
activity because the price of money in terms of
interest rates is very, very low. Now, I can't tell you
exactly how exaggerated their business characteristics are, but since it's hard to say that means it's
not conducive to analysis. We'd just rather not play
in that particular sandbox.*

Brian, you've got a number of foreign
companies in the fund. Is that pretty typical
or is it just that there are some unique
opportunities right now? **ADAM**

*It is somewhat typical. We look at the world on
a global basis and there are several industries that
I think you just cannot limit your analysis to the
borders of the U.S. and then forget about the rest of
the world. Pharmaceuticals are one area. Financial
services are another area. Automobiles are another area. Consumer electronics, although we don't
have any holdings there today, is another industry
where it's really necessary to look at the world on
a global basis. One of our bigger holdings right
now is GlaxoSmithKlein. That's a U.K.-based phar-
maceutical company but over half of their earnings
come from the U.S. and we think relative to other
companies here in the U.S. in pharmaceuticals it's
a very cheap stock for what it is.* **BRIAN**

Right now you've got about 40 stocks inside **ADAM**

the portfolio. When you go to sell something is it a function of you finding a 41st stock that's better than the 40th or is it just that a stock doesn't meet your criteria anymore and so you have to go look for something else?

BRIAN *That's a good question. It's really more the latter. We believe that over time the results of Cambiar Investors and the Cambiar Opportunity Fund are due to a very disciplined investment approach and that discipline relates primarily to how we manage our positions. Stocks sometimes get to a full valuation. What I mean by a full valuation is one where the financial characteristics of the company are really no longer consistent with the outlook and the risk/return characteristics become unfavorable. In other words, there is more downside risk than upside potential. At that point, a stock should be sold and we're not afraid to do that. In terms of the fund's size, we let the chips fall where they may. Typically we have somewhere between 36 and 44 holdings. I think we've averaged about 40 and we do not kick out a name just because we happen to have found a new name. If we find something that is very compelling and we have no specific sell candidates maybe we'll trim a little bit here, a little bit there, and squeeze in that new name. But what we've typically found as a matter of practice is that there are enough names leaving the portfolio as there are coming in and we* *don't generally need to squeeze one name out just to make room.*

Here's an important question that I ask every fund manager that I have on the show and that is, do you personally have money invested in your fund?

ADAM

Yes, I do. I personally have money invested in this fund. We have another Cambiar fund which is an international fund and I have roughly 40% of my liquid net worth between those two funds.

BRIAN

So you certainly care how the fund does?

ADAM

I care a lot. I have my own money in there. I have my kids' college money in there. I have plenty of exposure to Cambiar's funds.

BRIAN

Brian, your fund, the Cambiar Opportunity Fund, has beaten the market over the year to date, the one year, three year, and five year time horizons. I know you don't want to toot your own horn so I'll toot it for you, but what do you think is the key to your success?

ADAM

That's a good question. I mean it's been a heck of a streak. I think we have beaten the market six years in a row. Really I think the key is to be opportunistic and to be disciplined. Those are two important things that any fund manager has to do. You have to look at where value is and value

BRIAN

oftentimes is in places where people aren't looking or are negatively disposed towards. Which means one has to be willing to potentially underperform for a month or two on a given stock, or maybe even for a full year, to find stocks that are attractive valuations. The other thing that you have to do, and this is very important, is you have to remember to sell when things get full.

It's a nice fairy tale to believe that you are going to buy some little stock and it's going to grow and grow and management is going to be wonderful and ethical and it's going to do wonderful things and you are going to own it forever. Unfortunately, that and Cinderella and Snow White, those are all fairy tales. The reality is that the majority of companies come into the public marketplace, do well (hopefully) for a while, and oftentimes if they do particularly well the market bids the stock up to a valuation where it may be impossible for the stock to do well even if the company continues to perform well. We've been very good at remembering to sell. We've been very good at managing the positions and by doing that and doing it very judiciously and consistently we've been able to outperform the market and hopefully we can keep it up. I'm confident that we know what we're doing. Sometimes you get on a little streak and it isn't such a good streak, but we're confident we know what we're doing.

My guest on the show has been Brian Barish,   **ADAM**
manager of the Cambiar Opportunity Fund.
Brian, I want to thank you very much for being
with us, sharing part of your Saturday with us.

Thank you.   **BRIAN**

NTON SCHULTZ

Burnham Financial Services

ADAM   My guest on the show today is Anton Schutz. Anton is the manager of the Burnham Financial Services Fund and, as my regular listeners will know, this is a fund I have recommended to you over and over again. Anton, I want to thank you for taking the time to be with us today.

ANTON   *It's a pleasure to be with you today.*

ADAM   Aside from the excellent performance that you've delivered to my clients and to my listeners, one of the things that I like about your fund is the fact that you've got kind of a combination of some of the larger, more established financial services companies along with some smaller, perhaps regional banks, et ceteras, that are potentially takeover targets, right?

The Bold Truth About Mutual Funds

ANTON

That's absolutely right and there are times in the cycle where I'll tend to be more focused towards the smaller names if the valuations are right and there will be times in the cycle where I'll be more focused towards the larger names because again, their valuations are much more attractive. What I don't want to have happen is get to a point in the cycle where small caps are what I should own and I really can't because I can't get enough stock out there. So I really want to be able to preserve that opportunity.

ADAM

You have also launched two new funds: the Burnham Financial Industries Fund and the Burnham Long-Short Equity Fund. Tell me, how will the Financial Industries Fund be similar or dissimilar to your existing fund?

ANTON

Sure. The Financial Industries Fund is really going to be focused more on mid-size and larger companies, much more liquid. I think I have much more capacity to manage that portfolio and it will be focused more so on companies like AIG and Citicorp rather than Avington Savings Bank. So liquidity will not be an issue there. Again, there will be times in the cycle when that product may perform better and there will be times in the cycle where it will perform worse. But it'll be a pretty different product in terms of the types of liquidity and the types of names that it's going to be in. Actually to some extent we'll have more of an ability to write

covered calls because there'll be many more
names that actually have options on them.

ADAM   Now, what about the Long-Short Equity Fund?

ANTON   *Well, there are also points in the cycle where*
potentially you have a poor economy. You may
have rising rates; you may have inflation. It may
be very difficult to actually own financial services
stocks and you may be better off actually being on
the short side. Clearly, I've always viewed financial
services as a series of sub-sectors and generally
there is always a part of the sub-sectors where you
can make money on the long side. However, if
you had an environment of deflation you actually
would want to be in that sort. So I think this kind
of product won't work as well as the other funds in
some markets but clearly in a down market may
have some opportunity to outperform.

ADAM   So with that fund will you have the ability to go
100 percent long or 100 percent short?

ANTON   *Simplistically, not 100 percent short. You always*
have to have collateral for your shorts and in the
mutual fund world it's a little bit different than in
the hedge fund world. But yes, essentially I could
be net short such that the portfolio would benefit
from a general drop.

ADAM   The Federal Reserve has been raising interest

rates. Is there room for companies in the
financial services sector to make money?

Sure. Absolutely. Again, you have to look at the   **ANTON**
series of sub-sectors and the types of companies
that would actually benefit from a stronger econo-
my. If the Fed is raising rates it's raising rates
because the economy is overheating. You may
have a very strong capital markets environment.
Companies in the venture capital business are
probably going public so there may be large, large
gains out there for people who have equity posi-
tions in them. So broker dealers or money center
banks might be good places. Processing banks like
Bank of New York or State Street or Melon might
be good places. The E-brokers like an E-Trade or
an Ameritrade might be good places, so you've got
to look at the capital markets. Then, even if you
look at insurance as a sub-sector, you can talk
about companies like mortgage insurers. The mort-
gage insurers have had a tough time because their
insurance keeps going away because people keep
refinancing their houses and houses keep appreci-
ating so they keep losing business. If rates actually
start to move up they're actually going to not
only keep business they've already written, they'll
actually be able to continue to do some new
purchase business and they'll actually be able to
grow their balance sheets and their earnings, and
those are all pretty cheap stocks. So those are

the kind of places that can benefit if you have a strong economy and rates are rising for that reason.

ADAM So I guess the message is that regardless of the economic environment there are certain kinds of business that still may do all right, other ones that won't and obviously you're somebody who has a pretty good idea of where to be and where not to be.

ANTON *Well, thank you. I mean there clearly are those types of opportunities and you really need to have the right macro view. You need to have the right view of interest rates, economic strength, loan growth, the shape of the yield curve; those all go into play and they really have to take a bottoms-up approach on the right names within each sub-sector.*

ADAM Anton, is there anything else that you'd like to share with my listeners?

ANTON *Well, I think that the equity markets continue to obviously have upside. I'm actually very excited about the accelerating pace of mergers and acquisitions in financial services and I think that we're going to see a number of deals announced in the next few months, particularly in financial services. I think we're going to see some very large transactions. We've already seen Fleet and*

Bank America and we've seen Bank One and JP Morgan. I think we're going to see quite a few more and we'll keep seeing the small ones consolidate. If indeed there is pressure on some companies because rates may rise, it may hasten their desire to sell and clearly we're still looking for the foreign buyer to emerge, whether it's Royal Bank of Scotland, which actually announced a deal today for a credit card company, or HSBC coming back in the U.S. I'm very excited about the merger and acquisition environment.

Well, I want to thank you again for the great job that you've done for my clients at the *Mutual Fund Store* and for the listeners to the *Mutual Fund Show*. It's been a real joy to have you as a manager for our clients.   **ADAM**

Well, thank you very much.   **ANTON**

I wish you the best of luck with your new ventures.   **ADAM**

I appreciate it.   **ANTON**

Strategic Asset Management System

"If you're going to take the risk of the market, you owe it to yourself to be in the best funds possible."

A SYNOPSIS OF THE METHODS USED BY THE
MUTUAL FUND STORE TO GUIDE CLIENTS
THROUGH THE INVESTMENT-PLANNING PROCESS.

STRATEGIC ASSET MANAGEMENT SYSTEM

When you invest your money, are you really prepared to sift through the over 14,000 mutual funds? Do you have the knowledge or time to properly allocate your money between stocks and bonds? Large company stocks or small? International or domestic? Do you have the resources to evaluate your portfolio and reallocate if necessary?

With more mutual funds than stocks traded on the New York Stock Exchange and the American Stock Exchange combined, mutual fund investing has become more of a challenge than ever. And, unless you are willing to make this a full time job, you may not be able to keep track of your portfolio properly.

The country's largest investors—corporate pension plans, state and local governments, major foundations and endowments have known this for a long time. These institutional investors routinely turn to professional money managers who have the research, resources, and time to sort out all the choices, make the most informed decisions based on investor needs, appropriately diversify a portfolio, and offer ongoing investment guidance.

And now, The Mutual Fund Store lets you do the same.

Our Strategic Asset Management System (SAMS) is an investment advisory service from The Mutual Fund Store. SAMS provides you with professional investment advice and a personalized investment strategy. It also gives you access to strategically selected portfolios that encompass a wide range of investment styles that are appropriately diversified to meet your investment needs.

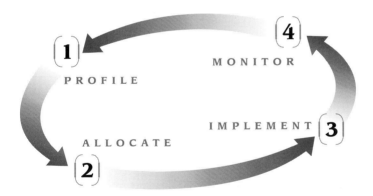

4 - S T E P   P R O C E S S

1. P R O F I L E . We recognize that every investor's situation is different and requires a recommendation based upon their own

unique circumstances. The first step of the SAMS process is an in-depth financial profile. We examine things like your time horizon, income requirements, risk tolerances and compatibility with your other investments.

2. A L L O C AT E . Based upon your individualized profile, our investment policy committee makes a specific asset allocation recommendation. This model is created by comparing the historical risk and reward performance of various asset classes to the parameters you have set. Because it is impossible to precisely time the market, your account will always be exposed to a variety of asset classes, though our proprietary model will attempt to overweight those classes about to go up, and give lesser weighting to those that have already moved.

3. I M P L E M E N T . We make a specific investment fund recommendation for each asset class. Our proprietary SAMS software allows us to screen from a database of more than 17,000 institutional money managers, load and no-load funds to find the very best professional manager for each asset type. While past performance is no indication of future gain, we believe that consistent superior performance is likely to continue.

4. M O N I T O R . This is probably the most important part of the process. First, you will receive an in-depth quarterly monitor which details the performance of your account for the current quarter, year-to-date, and since inception. In addition, we monitor the individual performance of the asset managers. We will recommend a management change if required for any reason. Also, we will make changes to the allocation model as market conditions warrant. Lastly, we will conduct an annual review to ensure that your model is still in line with your changing financial situation.

W H A T   I S   A S S E T A L L O C A T I O N ?   A N D   W H Y D O E S   I T   W O R K ?

T he purpose of an Asset Allocation Plan is to determine how your investment assets will be divided among the available investment alternatives. Our Asset Allocation recommendations are based on the Nobel prize-winning concepts of Modern Portfolio Theory—that through intelligent diversification you can protect against many investment risks. Gains in one investment may help offset losses in another.

No one can consistently predict the market's

THE IMPORTANCE OF ASSET ALLOCATION

PERCENTAGE OF RETURNS ATTRIBUTABLE TO VARIOUS FACTORS

Security Selection 5.66%

Asset Allocation 92.52%

Other 1.82%

next move, or which sectors will be in favor at any given time. The chart below illustrates the volatility of returns among different asset classes. Top-performing asset classes one year may be among the worst-performing the next year. Using our proprietary methods, we identify those asset classes showing the greatest promise for performance, and then develop an allocation plan that distributes your assets to those classes. We regularly monitor the allocation of your assets, and as conditions change, we re-evaluate and respond accordingly.

ANNUAL RETURNS FOR SELECTED ASSET CLASSES

	1997	1998	1999	2000	2001	2002	2003
BEST	Lrg Growth 36.54%	Lrg Growth 42.15%	NASDAQ 85.59%	Bonds 11.63%	Corp Bonds 8.44%	Gov Bonds 11.50%	NASDAQ 50.01%
	Lrg Value 29.99%	NASDAQ 39.62%	Lrg Growth 28.26%	Lrg Value 6.08%	Gov Bonds 7.23%	Corp Bonds 10.25%	Small Caps 58.54%
	Small Caps 22.36%	Internat'l 20.34%	Internat'l 27.31%	30 Day T-Bill 5.64%	Small Value -4.33%	Small Value -15.18%	Small Value 46.03%
	NASDAQ 21.62%	Lrg Value 14.68%	Small Caps 21.26%	Small Caps -3.03%	Lrg Value -5.99%	Lrg Value -15.52%	Internat'l 38.59%
	Bonds 9.68%	Bonds 8.67%	Lrg Value 12.73%	Internat'l -13.96%	NASDAQ 19.79%	Internat'l -15.94%	Lrg Value 31.79%
	30 Day T-Bill 4.87%	30 Day T-Bill 4.54%	30 Day T-Bill 4.44%	Lrg Growth -22.08%	Lrg Growth -20.42%	Lrg Growth -27.88%	Lrg Growth 25.66%
WORST	Internat'l 2.05%	Small Caps -2.56%	Bonds -0.83%	NASDAQ -39.29%	Internat'l -21.44%	NASDAQ -32.60%	Bonds 4.10%

It is important to keep in mind that the focus of this Asset Allocation model is based on your long-term objectives. It means taking a reasonable amount of risk in the expectation of higher returns. And, since time has a moderating effect on investment risk, the longer your investment time horizon the more likely you will earn a positive return.

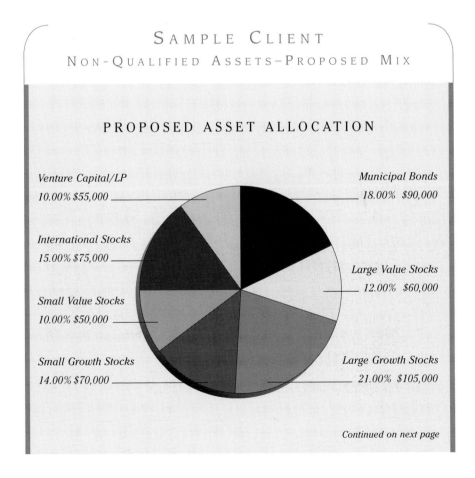

SAMPLE CLIENT
NON-QUALIFIED ASSETS–PROPOSED MIX

PROPOSED ASSET ALLOCATION

Venture Capital/LP
10.00% $55,000

International Stocks
15.00% $75,000

Small Value Stocks
10.00% $50,000

Small Growth Stocks
14.00% $70,000

Municipal Bonds
18.00% $90,000

Large Value Stocks
12.00% $60,000

Large Growth Stocks
21.00% $105,000

Continued on next page

Continued from previous page

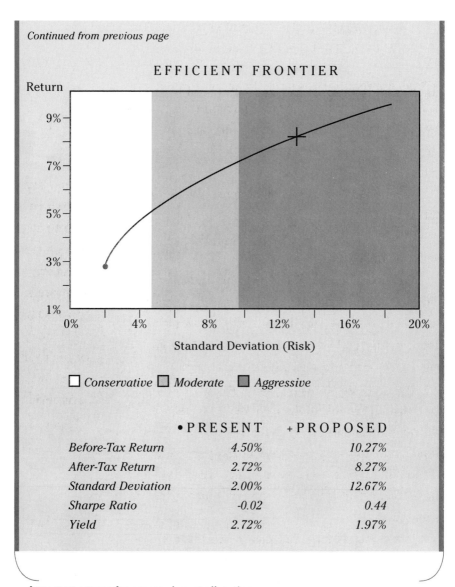

EFFICIENT FRONTIER

Return

□ *Conservative* □ *Moderate* ■ *Aggressive*

	• PRESENT	+ PROPOSED
Before-Tax Return	*4.50%*	*10.27%*
After-Tax Return	*2.72%*	*8.27%*
Standard Deviation	*2.00%*	*12.67%*
Sharpe Ratio	*-0.02*	*0.44*
Yield	*2.72%*	*1.97%*

Impact on returns for proposed asset allocation.

MUTUAL FUND SELECTION

S uccess requires research, analysis, insight. There are now more than 17,000 mutual funds available to investors. It seems there are hundreds of financial magazines and web sites, each with its own list of the funds you should buy.

At The Mutual Fund Store, we use the latest computerized tools to screen through the multitude of funds to identify those with the greatest opportunity for growth going forward.

Our screening process starts by analyzing the past performance of a fund relative to other funds of the same investment category. We identify funds whose performance has been in the top 20 percent of all funds of that type.

But, past performance is not the only factor to consider. For example, we look at the tenure of the fund's manager(s). While an individual fund's performance may have been spectacular, if the individual who is making the day-to-day investment decisions has changed, it is not the same fund.

It is certainly true that past performance is no guarantee of future results, however in the fund management business, like most other businesses, some people are just better at it than others. If a manager can demonstrate over extended periods of time that he can outperform

> IF YOU ARE GOING TO TAKE THE RISK OF THE MARKET, YOU OWE IT TO YOURSELF TO BE IN THE BEST FUNDS POSSIBLE.

PERFORMANCE PORTFOLIO SUMMARY
EXAMPLE

12/31/XXXX - 3/31/XXXX YEAR-TO-DATE

Beginning Value	244,120.86
Contributions	9,589.65
Withdrawls	(193.30)
Unrealized Gain (Loss)	13,334.52
Realized Gain (Loss)	312.81
Dividend Income	585.63
Interest Income	15.37
Management Fees	(991.23)
Ending Value	266,774.31
Investment Gain	13,257.10

12/31/XXXX - 3/31/XXXX YEAR-TO-DATE

	ACTUAL
Internal Rate of Return (Net)	5.23
S & P 500 Index	3.11
Nasdaq Composite Index	2.78
Dow Jones Industrial Average	3.24
MS EAFE (World) Index	2.60

4/1/XXXX - 3/31/XXXX TRAILING 12 MONTHS

Beginning Value	223,478.65
Contributions	9,589.65
Withdrawls	(193.30)
Unrealized Gain (Loss)	30,787.97
Realized Gain (Loss)	4,241.64
Dividend Income	1,961.10
Interest Income	60.02
Management Fees	(3,151.42)
Ending Value	266,774.31
Investment Gain	33,899.31

4/1/XXXX - 3/31/XXXX TRAILING 12 MONTHS

	ACTUAL
Internal Rate of Return (Net)	14.56
S & P 500 Index	11.91
Nasdaq Composite Index	12.02
Dow Jones Industrial Average	11.48
MS EAFE (World) Index	9.47

All returns net of fees

Information contained herein is based on sources and data believed reliable, but is not guaranteed. This is not an offer to buy or sell securities. This data is for informational purposes only and not intended to replace statements, confirms, or 1099 forms distributed by the custodian of your assets. Past performance does not guarantee future results. The Mutual Fund Store ADV is available upon request.

A sample report showing portfolio performance.

the vast majority of his peers, the likelihood is that it will continue going forward.

In addition, if a fund's performance begins to lag, or the manager leaves a fund, we reevaluate your holdings at that time. We will recommend a change, if necessary and appropriate.

There are many other factors to consider, as well. The point is that by using our proprietary selection process, we can help to increase the odds for superior performance.

WHY FEE-BASED SERVICE?

With SAMS you pay no commissions or loads to buy in, or to get out. You pay only a small percentage of the assets in your account.

There are three important reasons why we believe fee-based service is essential to a lasting adviser-client relationship:

1. You only pay for what you get. You pay only for the amount of time you use the service, as fees are prorated for the amount of time you have invested in the service.

2. Our goals are the same as your goals. Unlike traditional transactional brokers, we have no potential incentive to recommend trades for the sake of generating commissions. The only way we make more money is for your

money to grow so we get our little piece of a bigger number.

3. Our fee is all-inclusive. You know right up front exactly how much our services will cost, because the one fee includes everything from account maintenance to monthly statements. Schwab Institutional does charge short-term redemption fees and transaction fees on some mutual funds. Additionally, there may be commissions charged to liquidate individual stocks or bonds held in your account before The Mutual Fund Store begins management.

FEE SCHEDULE

Account Size	Quarterly Fee
$50,000-250,000	*0.375% on the first $250,000*
$250,001-500,000	*0.325% on the next $250,000*
$500,001-750,000	*0.275% on the next $250,000*
$750,001-1,000,000	*0.250% on the next $250,000*
$1,000,000	*0.225% on all additional assets*

Note: Fees above are in addition to internal management expenses charged by fund management. See prospectus for detail of these fees and expenses.

The Mutual Fund Store fee schedule as of publication date.

SUMMARY
OF SERVICES

What you get with a Mutual Fund Store Account:

o   Personalized Investment Consultation

o   Custom Allocation Model

o   Quarterly Reports

o   Ongoing Account Oversight

o   Professional Fund Selection

o   Coordination with Your CPA
    and/or Attorney

o   No Fee IRA Accounts

o   No-Load and Load-Waived Funds

o   Monthly Statement

o   Account Rebalancing

o   Optional Free Checking

o   Up to $150 million Account Insurance

o   Adam Bold & The Mutual Fund Store

THERE ARE TWO PARTS TO WHAT WE DO. INVESTMENT PERFORMANCE AND CLIENT SERVICE. OUR GOAL IS TO BE THE BEST AT BOTH.

THE MUTUAL
FUND STORE

The Mutual Fund Store client accounts are held by Schwab Institutional. Consolidation in one of these accounts simplifies the investing process and eliminates the need to contact each fund company individually.

The Mutual Fund Store is an independent full-service investment management and advisory firm with offices in major cities across the United States. Additional locations are being planned. We currently manage more than $1 billion for more than 5,500 clients.

The firm was founded through the desire of its founder and chief investment officer, Adam S. Bold, to provide clients with unbiased advice and cost-effective service.

Our goal is to provide the highest level of service and advice available anywhere, with a long-term outlook based on solid research, value, and common sense.

HELPFUL WEB SITES

www.Morningstar.com

The most comprehensive mutual fund website. The site allows you to see the performance, holdings and expenses of funds by ticker or name. It also features commentary and analysis of the mutual fund industry.

www.University.Smartmoney.com

A wonderful educational resource for novice investors. The site has a series of modules that explain the fundamentals of investing, as well as overall financial management.

www.FundAlarm.com

The site features the insightful monthly commentaries of Roy Weitz regarding all aspects of the mutual fund industry.

www.Smart401k.com

Co-founded by Adam Bold, this site allows participants in 401(k), 403(b) and other retirement plans to properly allocate and choose the best funds offered by their employer's plan. There is a small fee for using this service.

www.InvestorWords.com

This site offers a glossary of terms used in the financial services industry.

www.Brill.com

This site offers a collection of articles and opinions by various authors on retirement strategies, kinds of funds, fees, and more.

www.Investopedia.com

This site offers interesting articles about timely investment topics, as well as great articles for beginning investors.

www.FinanceCalc.com

A wonderful collection of financial calculators, including savings, retirement, college planning, and purchasing an automobile.

www.MutualFundShow.com

The official website for "The Mutual Fund Show," hosted by Adam Bold. You can listen to archived shows, as well as snippets sorted by topic, investment concepts, or specific mutual funds.

www.BankRate.com
This site tracks current interest rates for a variety of bank products, including home mortgages, credit cards, CDs, and automobile loans.

www.Money.CNN.com/funds

Mutual fund news, reviews, ratings, rankings, fund screeners and more from CNN & Money magazine.

www.MFEA.com

The official site of the Mutual Fund Education Alliance, an industry-supported organization dedicated to helping individual investors to understand mutual funds.

Martin Rosenberg, who assisted Adam Bold with this book project, has written extensively about finance, energy, technology and international business. His freelance work has appeared in the *New York Times*, *Seattle Times*, *Japan Times* and other publications.

He is editor-in-chief of *EnergyBiz*, a new national publication covering the energy industry, and previously was editor-in-chief of *Utility Business*, a monthly publication that won numerous journalism awards.

He was a business writer at *The Kansas City Star* from 1985-1998 and worked for newspapers in Oregon. He was a Fulbright Fellow to Japan, where he studied economics, and received a grant from the German Marshall Fund of the United States to study international agricultural issues.

He is a graduate of Reed College and holds a master's degree from Northwestern University's Medill School of Journalism. He and his wife, Matilda, reside in Kansas City and have three children.